D1271341

m

3250
.60B

OVID'S POETRY OF EXILE

OVID'S POETRY

The Johns Hopkins University Press
Baltimore and London

871
Ov40

OF EXILE

TRANSLATED INTO VERSE, BY
DAVID R. SLAVITT

© 1990 The Johns Hopkins University Press
All rights reserved
Printed in the United States of America

The Johns Hopkins University Press
701 West 40th Street
Baltimore, Maryland 21211
The Johns Hopkins Press Ltd., London

The paper used in this publication meets the minimum requirements of
American National Standard for Information Sciences—Permanence
of Paper for Printed Library Materials, ANSI Z3948–1984.

Library of Congress Cataloging-in-Publication Data

Ovid, 43 B.C.–17 or 18 A.D.
  [Selections. English. 1990]
  Ovid's poetry of exile/translated into verse by David R. Slavitt.
    p. cm.
  Translated from Latin.
  Contents: Tristia—Epistulae ex Ponto—Ibis.
  ISBN 0-8018-3915-7 (alk. paper).—ISBN 0-8018-3916-5 (pbk.)
  1. Ovid, 43 B.C.–17 or 18 A.D.—Translations, English. 2. Complaint
poetry, Latin—Translations into English. 3. Complaint poetry, English—
Translations from Latin. 4. Exiles—Poetry. I. Slavitt, David R., 1935–   .
II. Title.
PA6522.A2   1990
871'.01–dc20   89-45495
                                                                    CIP

CONTENTS

Prefatory Note   vi
Acknowledgments   ix

TRISTIA   1
   I   3
   II   27
   III   44
   IV   70
   V   92

EPISTULAE EX PONTO   117
   I   119
   II   143
   III   168
   IV   192

IBIS   223

1-19-94 Book House 2678

130277

These are very free renderings of Ovid's *Tristia, Epistulae ex Ponto,* and *Ibis.* What I was aiming for is a text that is lively and readable in English, and if that meant taking liberties, I allowed myself that privilege. After all, the Latin poems remain, and faithful, literal translations are available for those who wish to consult them.

It must be admitted, though, that these texts have not been very much consulted. The poems have not fared well, and my not altogether original explanation for their neglect—and even actual disesteem—is that the classics curriculum was established for the most part in the nineteenth century by British and German educators who were interested in molding character. Horatian stoicism is good for that; these poems of Ovid's are complaining, sometimes even whining, so they were not included among the usual offerings set for schoolboys to chew through. If anyone took notice of these works, it was only because Ovid wrote them, and then the usual posture was something between condescension and apology.

It was the self-pity of these neglected works that drew me to them—or, to put it another way, the bold and imaginative use to which the poet put his own biography for rhetorical and practical ends. The object of the poems was to try to get Augustus to relent and let him come home, or at least let him move to some place a little less remote than the frontier outpost to which he had been relegated.

Publius Ovidius Naso was born about 43 B.C. in Sulmo, prepared for a career in the law, but wound up as a poet. In A.D. 8 he was relegated by Augustus Caesar to Tomis, site of the present Constantza in Romania, near the mouth of the Danube. The publicly announced reason for this relegation (not an exile—his goods were never confiscated, and he retained his citizenship and, for better or worse, hope of reprieve) was the licentiousness of his *Ars Amatoria,* published ten years earlier. The more proximate cause of his banishment is not known. (For a lively discussion of the possibilities, see *The Mystery of Ovid's Exile* by John C. Thibault, University of California Press, 1964). For a twentieth-century reader, however, the arbitrariness of that banishment hardly needs explanation or elucidation. We have seen any number of writers—and nonwriters, too, for that matter—displaced and scattered around the earth, winding up in unlikely places where no one speaks their native language and wondering what there is they can do to recoup.

Ovid's scheme was to keep his name and the awareness of his plight alive back in Rome. Maybe Augustus might be persuaded to relent. He wrote these *Tristia* and sent back one volume a year to be circulated around the capital, where a friend might, perhaps, put in a good word to some under-secretary's assistant . . .

It was a good idea, but it didn't work. Augustus died, and Ovid was still out there in Tomis, scribbling away. He kept on with these letters, the only change being that in the *Epistulae*, the names of the recipients were not concealed. There was the hope that maybe Tiberius might be more amenable to persuasion, but Tiberius wasn't much interested. Ovid died in Tomis, still writing, still waiting for the news that never came.

It is a bleak and depressing story, but Ovid's spiritual and artistic resourcefulness are all the more admirable for that. We can recognize and understand his strength and courage better than did those nineteenth-century schoolmasters, for our century has, to our shame, better prepared us to understand capriciousness and violence. Ovid speaks to us across the millennia with an eloquent directness that seemed to me to require an urbanity and modernity that it has been my chief concern to achieve in this work. In order to undertake such a project, a translator must have at least the illusion of parity, must suppose himself to be a collaborator if not an actual pal of the poet who wrote the original work. When Ovid gets tiresome—as he seems to me on occasion to do—it is usually because he is showing off his erudition, piling myth upon myth, example upon obscure example. I understand his reason for doing this. Off on the shore of the Black Sea, in Tomis, a ridiculously primitive one-horse town (I suppose they had a horse), there were no libraries to consult, and the display of erudition was in itself a virtuoso act of defiance. But it can get wearisome for the modern reader, and when that happens, I invent what I need, usually reducing the number of references and expanding on those that remain, or sometimes enlarging upon something else in the poem. I have kept the same length and scale as in Ovid's poems.

In the *Ibis*, however, that piling of reference upon learned reference becomes, very quickly, funny. This is a poem of hatred that is also hilarious, the author in his remote helplessness being at least in part the butt of his joke. My model was that of elaborate Yiddish invective, which is often self-mocking. This is one of the few weapons left to those who are powerless and in exile. (It was Professor Gordon Williams who more or less dared me to undertake this curious poem, and I am grateful to him for having set me this delightful task.)

It was a comfort to live like a schoolboy and do my Latin every morning, and I shall miss Ovid. I am pleased, as I look back on these pages, to see how my high-handed and even irresponsible approach (which is how some classicists view the intrusion of poaching poets) has produced what seems to me essentially Ovidian. I have introduced very little and I have kept to his tropes and turns, his timbres, his gestures. What Ovid wrote was primarily a poetry of dramatic gesture, assuming a persona that I have also tried to assume. I have tried, in other words, to *be* Ovid. This was a crazy thing to attempt, I freely admit, but then all translation is crazy, perhaps because some such miraculous transformation is always what is required.

It is not for me to judge how successful I may have been in my imposture, but without immodesty I think I can confess how, for some years, it has been a delight and a solace to imagine myself as Ovid in exile. With the work now at an end, I am sensible of a painful diminution.

Acknowledgments

The author wishes to express his appreciation for a grant from the National Endowment for the Arts which enabled him to work full time on the translation of the *Epistulae Ex Ponto*, and his gratitude to the Rockefeller Foundation for a Bellagio Center residence for the translation of the *Ibis*.

The author and the Johns Hopkins University Press thank Bell-flower Press of Cleveland, Ohio, for permission to reprint the *Tristia*.

Finally, the author is grateful to *Chronicles, Southwest Review, Texas Review*, and *Classical Outlook*, the journal of the American Classical League, in which some of the *Epistulae* have appeared.

TRISTIA

FOR ISAAC

And if his yowl
demands the whole world, who is to say
he has not the right?

BOOK I

I, 1

Little book, you're off to town without me, wet
    behind the ears (your ink is hardly dry).
Enjoy it. I can't go. Papa's not allowed.
    But for your old man's sake, a little restraint:
no fancy cover tarted up with dyes, no gaudy
    title page done up in colored inks,
and none of those fancy deckle edges or gold leaf
    for your pages. You're in mourning. Better look it,
bereaved to be believed. It's probably worth a try.
    If you could sprawl on the page messily, blotches
strewn around in the text, suggesting teardrop stains . . .
    It isn't sentimental; what's sentimental
is getting your audience wrong, attributing to them
    more taste and shrewdness than what they've got.
Go little bookaroo, and with words from my lips
    say how-do-you-do to the places I remember
gladly. You will dance there (ho-ho) with my feet.
    If somebody there should still remember me
and ask how I am, you tell them I'm alive. Not well,
    and not happy (there's no need to lie),
but say that I hold the mere fact of life as a gift.
    For him who asks more, let him read your pages.
Be circumspect, yourself—as I should have been. Remember
    I am a criminal sent here into exile.
I'm likely to be reviled. The best defense is silence,
    and there isn't, in this case, a lot to say,
or nothing a clever lawyer would be able to think up.
    What you do is look for those who don't
attack, who seem sympathetic to me and maybe to you,
    the ones who will read our elegiac lines
and pause every now and then to get control of a voice
    that nearly cracked, or the ones who rub their eyes

that aren't tired but nevertheless glisten. To them
 nothing need be said. They wish us well
with a silent prayer that Caesar may somehow yet relent—
 which I answer here with a like prayer
that they may be spared such torments who already have felt
 generously, vicariously, my pain.
Amen to both our prayers. It isn't death I fear
 but death here and a grave at the end of the world.
But I digress—or do I? Your main task and the only
 reason I brought you into the world was to plead.
Ugly as you are, you'll limp, sidle, wheedle,
 smile, and fawn for me. And back in Rome,
they'll look at you with disdain. This from Naso? Yes,
 and for Naso! Let them look to your brothers
and then consider the circumstances of your creation.
 Poetry should come from a mind at peace,
not this cabin, these rough winds, this boiling surf,
 these scudding clouds, doom and omens of doom.
Who can write in fear or think clearly in fear?
 At any moment the door may open to guards,
or hired thugs, or robbers, daggers or swords in hand.
 It's not far-fetched. But to write this way,
that's far and clumsily fetched. Let them know
 what this room was like where I begat you.
Homer's talent burdens every poet, but I
 must emulate his blindness. And add to that
a kind of deafness: my ears thirst for Latin's supple
 elegance; here all I hear are grunts.
At least you're free of one worry most books have
 (and poets): the love of fame, the hope of pleasing,
the craving for honor and fortune . . . It's like a game for children
 for which I remember the rules and strategy but
cannot quite recall the point of it. Why bother?
 Why expend attention on such trifles?

Back then, in my old life, I played as hard
        as any poet, imagined marble busts
with my features, phrases of my own composition
        chiseled into the pediments of buildings
glowing in snowy marble . . . What has happened to that
        unoriginal fancy? It is enough
that I don't hate poetry now, that I still write,
        despite how it has injured me. Booko,
would that we could exchange places, that I could go,
        my own book, to the city. It won't be easy.
You won't come as a stranger, some amusing exotic
        from one of the provinces. Even without a title,
your style—mine—will proclaim to anyone who can read
        who and what you are and where you come from.
Therefore you'll be blamed for the sins of your elder brothers,
        by fools who will snipe: "Another dirty book?"
Tell them to read your title. Try not to lose your temper.
        The Art of Love wasn't so bad a book,
and we have already paid the penalty for its sins.
        Watch yourself on the slippery Palatine,
that eminence from which the thunderbolt struck me down,
        the hill where Caesar lives. Mercy is there,
but still I fear the place where I was stricken. The dove,
        once wounded, dreads the hawk's wingbeat;
the lamb, saved from the mauling wolf, won't stray from the
                                                    flock.

        Every man of the Argive fleet who survived
the Capherean rocks gave the Euboea a wide berth—
        not that they all turned coward, but one learns
mortality. Good luck doesn't come with a guarantee.
        As Icarus showed us, flying high is fun
but risky. Watch it. Learn from my reverses
        how to hold back, how to wait for your moment.
Let someone introduce you before you make your approach.
        If anyone can lighten my burden, Caesar

can if he choose: he is divine Achilles to my
      Telephus—only the man who gave the wound
is able to cure it. Still, go easy. My hope is small;
      my fears are great before that power. It sleeps.
Take care not to rouse it again—for pity's sake.
      You're going home. Not just back to Rome
but to a particular street, a particular house, a room,
      a space on the shelf beside your brothers' spaces.
Some will display their titles openly. But three,
      the volumes of *The Art of Love*, will hide
like Telegonus or Oedipus, those parricides.
      Keep clear of them. But *The Metamorphoses*
greet in my name. Let them know how I've changed myself,
      as different from then as you are different from them.
Joy, promise, hope, they all metamorphose into
      mockeries of what they were. The one
good fairy in Pandora's box isn't hope
      but numbness, and one learns to pray for that.
Oh, I have more instructions, commissions, and advice.
      I could write it all down. It'd be a book
as long as you are. I mustn't keep you waiting further.
      Let me not burden you more, nor him that bears you,
nor them that I hope shall read you, nor their gentle hearts.
      The road is long. Square your shoulders. March.
Remember who you are and what I was, and am,
      here at the end of the earth. The gods be with you.

I, 2

There was rain all afternoon and the wind was rising; now
      the storm's rage has reached its height. Lightning

flashes our peril at us. The day was dark but the night
    blazes. Fish that could fly would be able to breathe
in these thick torrents. The rain assaults us as in anger.
    A little bit of rain and wind is fine,
would have suited my mood and fortunes. But this is excessive:
    my self-pity has given way to terror,
as poetry, hours ago, to increasingly fervent prayer.
    Ye gods of sea and sky, give me a break!
It isn't fair to conspire. You used to balance out.
    Vulcan favored the Greeks, and Apollo the Trojans;
Venus helped the Teucrians when Pallas was working against
                            them.
    I've got Caesar's wrath already upon me.
What is the point of your punishing me as well?
    It's ganging up, the way schoolchildren do.
When Neptune hounded Ulysses, Minerva helped him out,
    saving him from her own uncle. Uncle!
I give up! O gods, I am not worthy of this
    particular attention. Where is the god
whose help will restore the balance in this melodramatic plot?
    It just doesn't make sense. I'm not a hero
whose death in the last act will produce any feelings of awe.
    Nobody's even paying any attention
It's comedy, right? Or farce! So where is the happy ending?
    It's hard to pray in weather like this. The rain
isn't only falling into my mouth, but rising,
    blowing up my nose. I have cried out,
have hollered loud as I could. But the wind takes my words
    and whips them away. The gods are unable to hear
what I can hardly hear, myself. I try to look upwards
    but the sea's billows heave the ship about
so that *upwards* becomes a myth we no longer believe in.
    What is the helmsman steering for, I wonder?
Into the wind? The winds circle like wild beasts
    massing upon an ox. There are no stars.

I can no longer feel the rail I am clutching so hard.
    Can the helmsman do more than hold onto the tiller
as I grasp at this railing? Is there any intention left?
    Dare I pray for the only calm there is,
fathoms deep below this buffeted fragile keel?
    My wife grieves for me, sent into exile.
She has no idea I may never live to see it. I
    was right to leave her behind, high and dry.
To suffer the fury of wind and water is bad enough
    without the burden her innocent uncomplaining
company would be. The storm is like a siege
    with the waves trying to stave in the ship
with blows from its catapult. We're all going to die,
    but there's supposed to be a death-bed scene
with friends and loved ones leaning to hear my last words.
    Fish will give me my only farewell kiss.
But what about the rest, the officers and crew
    and the other passengers, all of them innocent?
Should my taint affect them? They have done nothing
    (not that what I've done deserves all this).
It's crazy! My punishment has already been decided.
    If Caesar wanted to kill me, he'd have said so
and it would have been done there. To send me away, as he did,
    was mercy. I can appeal a sentence of exile,
or he could change his mind. But not if I'm drowned now.
    What is the point? Aren't my woes enough?
What do you want with me? Pick on somebody else,
    a trader who uses the winds and plows the seas
with merchandise for gain. Or choose a student, young
    and cocky, bound for Athens, full of himself
and his high hopes . . . I was one of those happy youngsters
    ages ago. Did you spare me then for this?
Look, if you let me go, I continue on into exile.
    What's the satisfaction in killing me

compared to a much more noble person, or one more vile?
　　Someone on his way to Alexandria,
pluck him up and save him from all those extravagant vices.
　　Give me a calm sea and a fair wind,
and I can go to Romania. Has a more modest prayer
　　ascended to heaven any time this month?
The wild shore of the Black Sea is my destination.
　　It's not a request worth a divine refusal.
Sensible men pray to live to see Rome,
　　but I am asking only to get to Sarmatia,
and gargle when I should be eloquent. Gods, listen!
　　I take it back. I've been doing it wrong.
If you want to be mean and punish, calm the winds and water
　　and speed the vessel toward its destination.
There a lonely exile, stretching out in time
　　as bleak as the terrain itself, as vast, as empty,
waits to nibble my life away, a day at a time,
　　toying with me just as a cruel cat
will toy with a mouse. Spare me that and kill me now.
　　Wreck the ship. Or leave it and take only me,
washing me overboard with a wave as big as that last one.
　　Is it the ninth wave or the one after
we're supposed to fear? And where are the other eight,
　　the gentle ones? You could be gentle, you know,
excuse me from the sentence that Caesar laid upon me,
　　and grant me death's reprieve. You know my fault—
no guilt attached to a deed more stupid than evil.
　　You who know all can erase the decree
and me with it. In Rome, I was always loyal to Caesar,
　　to him and his house, have offered up incense,
have tried to serve him well, praising his ordered state
　　and showing others how to thank and praise.
If I'm not telling the truth, then let the next wave take me.
　　The sea still thrashes like a madman,

but even madmen tire. The pitching is less severe.
        There, in the east, the gloom begins to shred,
to fray a little. The wind is mournful more than angry.
        The storm subsides. The ship is likely to make it.
Do I give thanks to the gods for harkening to my prayer,
        or bite my tongue for having betrayed me again?

I, 3

When night falls here, I think of that other night
        when the shadow fell once and for all and I
was cast out of the light into this endless gloom.
        Twilight here calls forth from certain birds
a kind of mournful twitter, but silent tears from me
        as I think of how it was that night in the city.
The nimble hours skittered, turning us all clumsy
        and the simplest menial task onerous. Packing
was either a nightmare itself or one of those cruel jokes
        you sometimes find in your worst dreams. Papers
hid and even after we'd found them refused to stay put.
        We blamed ourselves for having wasted time
trying to talk it out and ourselves into understanding
        what was going on, and not to impose
what we were feeling. I'd made lists of clothing, equipment . . .
        But who had the composure? And pitiless time
nudged us along, forcing our minds to these cruel questions.
        Or was it, perhaps, a mercy? We managed to laugh
once or twice, as my wife found in some old trunk
        odd pieces of clothing. "This might be
just the thing this season, the new Romanian mode . . . "
        And just as abruptly our peal of laughter would catch

and tear into tears as she dropped the preposterous shepherd's
cloak
and we held each other. On drill, like a legion,
the minutes passed, each of them bearing Caesar's blazon,
advancing by so much the terrible deadline.
It wasn't the fall of Troy, but what we all dread
as we read of the fall of Troy, whatever the scale
by which we figure grief, investing in those old figures
what our approximate hearts have learned to feel.
It was grief, as if I had died. But there I was, alive,
adding to that grief—so it was worse.
I remember the silence—not only of men and women but
dogs—
and crossing the courtyard, I happened to notice the moon,
which seemed to slide past clouds with the same oily silence.
The street in front of the house that hour was silent
as the Capitol hill nearby: no light, no shout, no runner
bearing reprieve or pardon. The temples were quiet
as vacant houses. Or tombs. Or the echoes of all my prayers.
To a man of words it's appalling, the realization
that argument and persuasion fail, the craft of a lifetime.
There was no way to speak to that terrible silence.
Caesar knew the distinction between a crime and my blunder
but with a single word he had undone
all my words and turned me into a dumb beast
that endures its rain of blows until the gods
speak for it and soothe its master's distracted spirit.
My wife sobbed at the hearth, her hair streaming
down as if the flood from her eyes were insufficient,
and wailed to the household gods. What could I say?
Before her, too, I was a dumb beast.
Even the darkness, friend to lovers and thieves,
deserted me at the last and left me to face the dawn
and its stern command. My every tender feeling

turned against me—my love of my wife, home, country—
    jailors now and torturers. The bear
spun on her tail, a beast performing tricks in a circus,
    and faded away as by a kind of magic,
cruel rather than gay. I took the first step
    with which all journeys are said to begin
but could not take the second. I turned back, unable
    either to move out through the door or back
into the house. I was barely able to breathe or see.
    For the sake of appearance I thought up some instruction,
a last minute suggestion. My wife nodded agreement
    but then renewed her plea that I take her along.
One more time, I rehearsed what we'd already gone over—
    and I still don't know whether I can believe it
or if she does or ever did, that her staying in Rome
    could do me more good, could do us both
more good than her coming along to join me in exile.
    I set forth again, or like some drunk
watched in an unconnected way how my feet progressed
    one and then the other. Behind me, she fell
rolling upon the floor. Her hair swept into the hearth
    stirring the dust and ashes. I would have turned
back, but my feet having learned the independent knack
    kept on going. I heard her call my name
as if I were one of the mourners in my own funeral train.
    I thought I'd survived the worst. What could be worse?
But my wife arose, pursued me, held onto me, weeping.
    What Mettus, the traitor, felt when the teams of horses
hitched to his arms and legs, tore him apart, I felt.
    The difference is that his pain wasn't mixed with love.
Servants pulled her away. I felt where she had clutched me,
    the places on my arms and my neck burning.
I tried to hold the fading sensations. I wanted to keep them
    exactly as they'd been at that awful moment,

but even pain betrays us, faithless, fading away.
  A third time, I started forth, my feet
no longer a wonder. Now, worse than a drunk,
  a sleepwalker marching into his nightmare,
I negotiated the street and managed to reach the corner.
  A man can lose his life in different ways:
it bleeds out or flies away in that last gasp.
  But to walk away from a life . . . I've no idea
whether it's harder or not, but I cannot suppose the dead
  desire still to die, that the suffering stop.
I never had anything like it happen—so that survival
  was something to be ashamed of. Only a brute
could have kept on walking and living past that corner.
  Whatever worth there was in me died there.

I, 4

Another pitching ship: the water sluices down
  the painted god's face gracing the transom,
while the crew is grim, resigned. This is the life they know.
  If one storm has spared them, this or the next
may not. But the end is clear. They understand they have chosen
  a life, a death. I, too, am impassive,
a dead man excused from fear as well as hope.
  We're all—I begin to see—in the same boat.
The sea is running heavy. Canvas cracks and the mast
  creaks in a lower register. The helmsman
keeps her into the wind, taking her where she'll go,
  a rider upon a horse he can't control.
It has happened often before, and mostly patience triumphs,
  but we've been blown so far off course that the winds,

if they hold, are likely to take us back to that inviting
    Italian coast on which I may not set foot.
An elaborate practical joke—to travel all this time
    and wind up where I hope and fear we might.
I'd though I'd passed those straits and put the shallows behind.
    I'd thought I had learned the sailors' acquiescence.
The shrouds whine and the spars squeak their unending
                                  complaint,
    but the men keep still. To learn to admire patience
is easy; patience itself is hard, and the sea a demanding
    mistress. There's no end to the business of learning
how not to be a child, tired, hungry, cold,
    and calling for his mama. Not to call . . .
that's the beginning of courage. But not even to care
    is either folly or wisdom and faith in the gods.

I, 5

I am pained to think how friendship ought to proclaim itself—
    as mine for you cannot. To join my name
to yours would be to do you much disservice. My taint
    may, like sickness, spread. I therefore embrace
but cover my mouth and turn my face away. Still,
    you know who you are and what I owe you, second
to none of all my friends. That "all" sounds like a lot.
    A handful, I should say. An exquisite few
who didn't cut out—as I nearly tried to do, myself.
    Suicide's drastic cure for all of my ills
began to look more and more attractive, but you were there,
    an imperturbable help. As long as I live,

I shall remember how your selflessness restrained me
从 from the wrong kind of selflessness. Some good
is supposed to come puffing from the worst of ill winds.
        From my catastrophe, I've learned to value
a friendship such as yours—and there aren't many. I pray
        the occasion may never arise in which your need
is as great as mine was; may you never come to feel
        such gratitude or understand what I'm saying.
The sailor never knows how seaworthy is his vessel
        until a storm has tried it. The commonplace
wisdom that we suspect or resist turns out to be true.
        The poets have always known it. All great friendships
pass through refining flames that separate the dross
        from the precious gold. Think of mad Orestes
and Pylades, or of Euryalus and Nissus, dying
        together. Never mind counting on my fingers;
I can reckon on my ankles the friends who haven't
        dropped away as I sank like a stone.
Rats from a sinking ship. Fortune's friends, not mine.
        I know all the formulas and recite them,
but still it doesn't feel good. I can't even blame them
        for behaving that way, saving themselves
distress and inconvenience. That's what people do.
        That you and a couple of others are different keeps me
from utter despair not only for myself but for us all,
        for what we call with vain pride The Human
Condition. I tell you that Rome's fora, her arches and temples,
        are standing on illusions rather than hills.
The rude huts around me, their occupants always armed,
        even to make the short trip to the outhouse—
these are the temples to truth and man's place in the cosmos.
        I thought for a time there were practical reasons, fear
not least among them—that would excuse a lot.
        Fear lest the emperor's anger ruin

reputations and fortunes. That could have prompted caution
    on the part of all those people I used to drink with.
But they were wrong. Their fears were groundless. It wasn't
                            prudence
    after all but pusillanimity.
Nothing has happened to you. The emperor is not
    vindictive, has often praised an opponent's valor
on the field of battle. In Rome, among his own people,
    how could he value character any less?
Those former friends, for fear of insulting Caesar Augustus,
    treat him as if we were crazy, stupid, or both.
He isn't—as you always knew and have demonstrated.
    I wish I could figure a way to contrive the right
endings for everybody as the literary tradition,
    teasing us, offers (but to our benefit
or harm? I wish I knew). Those lick-spittle sycophants
    would all be banished while you'd be richly rewarded—
and I'd be recalled, of course. Thus, I torment myself;
    like a daydreaming child, I imagine how
it ought to be. It doesn't do anyone any harm
    and it passes the time, the heaviest burden I have.
Ulysses' travels were awesome, and we all learned to admire
    such heroic endurance. But I'm no hero,
and my lot is worse than his: he was going home,
    while I have fled mine; he was a warrior,
while I am a gentle soul, used to the comforts of life;
    he could rely on his own strenuous efforts,
while I must complain to my wife and hope that a few friends
    may speak in my behalf. But the worst of it is
that he was invented. Homer understood from the start
    that beyond all the adventures, Ithaca waited;
my fate is not so clear, nor is there any convention
    forcing my author toward a happy ending.
It's hard, my friend, hard. And although it must seem unlikely,
    I do try to be brave and silent. Days

and weeks go by and I've done well, and then some random
    thought will undo me, a chance association
reduce me to helpless tears. Read between the lines,
    between the letters—there you'll find my pain.

I, 6

Let us imagine a ruin—say, of some small Greek temple
    in an out of the way place, where the god happened
to speak or spare or warn or simply to show herself,
    nearly leveled, say by an earthquake, but one
single column left, still holding up its corner
    by which we can imagine the rest of the structure.
Which is the more affecting, the ruined part of the building,
    or that surviving piece of it, forlorn,
bereaved of the rest? My life is the ruin; yours, dear wife,
    is that still-standing beautiful pillar, vessel
for the spirit that yet abides. How else to declare
    my love for you, who deserve a less wretched
though not a better or more adoring husband? My powers
    are not what they were. Clumsy sincerity
must speak with its thick tongue, stammering out thanks
    and affection, unadorned but still heartfelt.
I know how you've been besieged, from the very day I left.
    Here the wolves creep close and the vultures circle,
eager for easy pickings. Back in Rome, gallants
    came with offers of comfort no less rapacious
than predator or scavenger would have been.
    Another Penelope, you fended them off—
for which your fame should exceed hers. At any moment,
    her husband might have reappeared, but you

have no such comforting hope, not even as idle fancy.
    But I'm no Homer. I never was,
even when I was a poet good enough to offend
    the august powers. Now I'm a picturesque
ruin, a possible asset to Tomis for the tourists
    I might attract to inspect my bleak wreck
and picnic here. Let them come and take the tour.
    As guide, I shall recite to them the marvel
of your faith and love to which I am monument.
    No triumphal arch that looms in Rome
stands prouder. Let the world come to admire,
    as I have learned to do, now and forever.

I, 7

I can imagine plaster figurines that grace
    library niches, a bust of mine among them . . .
Tear its wreath away: its ivy ought not mock
    my bare original. Rather let it bear
whatever the heavens mete out, as I am schooled to do.
    Or better, let me suppose a particular friend
who still may wear my likeness in gold upon his finger.
    But the distance between us grows each day as flesh
wears with cares his metal will never deign to show.
    Of all memory's tricks, the most cruel
is accuracy: from those who remember me the clearest,
    I am the furthest exiled. Tasting my own
medicine of metamorphosis, I change
    into something poor and strange, learning
otherness and difference as if for the first time.
    That old manuscript of mine, unfixed,

fixes me, skewered like some kind of rare bug.
     That's as bad as anything I can think of—
readers judging the work unfairly, as if it were finished
     rather than interrupted by my abrupt
departure. A poor advocate, I plead my poem's
     sad case (and to better effect, I hope,
than I pled mine). It would have been a mercy had I
     put it into the stove with my own hand
rather than leave it exposed to the weather of good taste.
     But copies beyond my reach turned against me,
accusers. Yet like any parent, I can forgive them,
     even proud that they can command attention
and prosper in the world. Let them please their readers
     from whom I crave indulgence rather than praise.
I wish—again as a parent—the poem were better, that I
     had made it better, had known what a life-and-death
matter it was and is. I've lost that old brashness
     and like as not the skill too. Still,
I wish I could add to that poem of mine, just a few lines:
     "What you read here, the poet never published.
Rather, it survived what might be called his death.
     All poems are written in that shadow
and harsh light, as I know now. Forgive my defects,
     but mourn my virtues and their stern demands."

I, 8

Backward shall rivers flow from the sea to their upland sources
     while the wheeling sun careens from west to east;
water itself shall burn and flame sweat waterdrops,
     the laws of nature reversed or—worse—revoked.

When whim is the only rule, nothing is sure or likely
      or unlikely—so that all our wisdom
is undone and we all are infants again, groping
      in a huge, incomprehensibly dangerous world.
I'd sooner expect that than what has in fact happened—
      which feels as bad and leaves me just as bewildered:
A friend on whom I had counted, to whom I had looked to help
      has turned away. There was no fixity
surer than that friendship—and none mattered so much.
      O perfidious! Did you just forget me?
Or was it fear to approach, lest I might prove contagious?
      Or was it distate? Disaster *is* distressing.
But for your own sake, to think of yourself as kind,
      decent, loyal, and so on, could you not
feign conventional sorrow, mouth the commonplaces,
      copy out the copy-book phrases and send them
with smug relief as much as regret? I don't understand . . .
      What can one man know of another's heart
unless he look into his own, considering how he'd feel
      were the circumstances reversed. To see your face
once more, and to say "Farewell" for the last time . . .
      How could I fail to do that much—or little—
if you were the one leaving? Other people showed up,
      acquaintances, people I hardly knew, strangers.
And in some of their faces I saw the glistening eyes of grief
      as they watched me board, leaving behind the life
you knew so well, the life we'd shared. Nothing! The wind
      blew it away like chaff. But even the wind
from the right quarter can sting tears from the coldest eye.
      The landscape here ought to be yours, the bleak
prairie, the rocky crags, the hills with their veins of flint,
      this ill-omened terrain so far from Rome.
We took for granted the narrow streets whose paving stones,
      worn smooth by civilized feet, seem jewels

from where I'm standing now. I can remember nights
  of long carouse and walking home at dawn
(it must have rained in the small hours and then cleared)
  when the stones gleamed in the moment's light. And you,
reading this will suppose that I've turned sentimental
  and a little foolish. But do not condescend
as the living often do when they think of the baleful dead.
  It isn't our mute reproach that's hard to bear
but sentiment, forgiveness, and love—which can be weapons
  or instruments of torture. Knowing this,
how can I not forgive you, affirm our old friendship,
  and recall with pleasure how it once gleamed?

I, 9

A long and happy life! I wish you what you will
  and, further, that it turn out to be as good
as it appeared in anticipation. The best there is
  is what you ought to have. I frame my prayer
on your behalf with more care than I ever gave
  when I addressed the cruel gods on my own
sad hook. Prosper! I wish you that, my friend,
  not only for prosperity's sake but friendship's,
most friends being—believe me—fair weather,
  which is still better than none at all. This isn't
what you want to hear, I'm sure. May you never learn
  the truth at first hand, how when the cloud
darkens your skies they flee away into their holes
  Most men are shadows, dogging the footsteps
of elongated figures on whom the sun's golden rays
  happen to shine and are just as faithless. But you

aren't like that, can hardly believe that most men are,
    or that your own behavior is rare. So gems,
if they thought at all would think themselves like any stones,
    having no idea of dull. But here,
dull, dun, and dreary, as far as the eye can see,
    conspire to remind me of your worth.
When I was my old self, before this nightmare started,
    my house was crowded with guests, my table's places
as full as my heart with affection I supposed was returned
    and mutual—for who would doubt his friends?
But when the blow came, how many turned away?
    One of those who didn't, you may reckon
how few remained. The accounting will not take you long.
    Did all of them dread the thunderbolt whose power
destroys whatever is near? But Caesar himself approves
    loyalty, steadfastness . . . as Hector approved
Patroclus who was loyal to his friend, the mighty Achilles.
    There are many such stories I could cite
except that I fear to write the legendary names
    for my words seem to drain away feeling,
leaving the hearts of men indifferent and unmoved.
    Just as my tears freeze here in the cold,
my sometime friends' eyes are dry and their hearts icy
    at a recitation of sufferings not ancient,
not of demigods, but mine, here, now.
    Still, in my distress, I find some respite
in the news of your good fortune which somehow speaks to my
                                    child's
    notion of what's fair—to see that virtue
can sometimes be rewarded, that grace can still attend
    the graceful and the gifted. I told you once
what a great stage your gifts required for their own
    proper play and the city's benefit.
Not from the sheep-guts or flights of birds or lightning-
    flashes on my left did I divine this,

but reasoned how it ought to be—and sometimes is.
    Some lives that seem to fit a pattern
let us suppose a world of cause and effect, of just
    deserts, let us remember how as children,
gentled by fair and loving parents we snuggled down
    in pleasant dreams—from which I have been waked
rudely, my friend, and I blink and rub my eyes in the dark,
    trying not to cry. I hear your voice,
reassuring, familiar, as if from the dream itself,
    and I take a deep breath and do feel better.
Prosper, then, and continue to speak as I have heard you,
    to me and about me back in Rome,
unsaying the many foolish things I said and wrote
    to get here in the first place, rousing me
at last from this long and bad dream that I've been having,
    rising, however distant, like the sun.

I, 10

A poet's journey, ajingle with all those proper names,
    the gold coins of the language: the Gulf of Corinth
and Isthmus, Cenechreae, Imbros, Samothrace,
    the Zerynthian shore where Hecate kept house
in a cave, the Hellespont, Dardania, Lampsacus
    where Venus bore that lucky stiff, Priapus . . .
Wonderful fun, although a little showy, the boast
    not being that one had actually gone
to all those places but rather a library, one's
    own or a friend's or patron's. I still feel
sneezy at some of those names or the smell of dust in the scrolls
    where I first found them. And for such ostentation,

the gods punish me, take me by the reluctant hand
    and drag me past each of these outlandish
improbable places. It's life exaggerating art
    and turning it into a cruel joke. I'd written
of the realm of the goddess of Hunger, a barren and icy place
    in furthest Scythia—to which I go,
metamorphosed myself by a clever bureaucrat
    or else by a pure and mindless coincidence
in which one is tempted—or driven—to read the machinations
    of the serious gods themselves. I have yet to pass
the famous straits that separate Sestos and Abydos,
    to escape the dreaded Symplegades that crash,
chewing up unlucky ships—but they'll spit me out,
    for I have been reserved for a worse fate,
a long slow dwindle in Tomis, that huddle of mean
    hovels in the chill wind that blows
off the dark Euxine, out of the northeast
    five days in a week. They are all lessons
in presumptuousness, names scribbled on maps as if
    to fill their empty spaces. The world's spaces
are empty as ever, producing a kind of horizontal
    vertigo at the awful expanse of space
that fades away to the shimmering line that can't fend off
    the sky's larger emptiness from our own.
Space fills the darkness. The last leg of my journey
    awaits me—Apollonia, Dionysopolis.
At least they know by what god they have been forsaken,
    but so do I. Still, if I reach Tomis,
I'll sacrifice a lamb, offering up to Minerva
    all I can afford in the way of thanks.
And you, Castor and Pollux, friend to all who sail,
    protect the ship, send us a fair wind,
and keep us from the bottom, the emptiest space of all
    where the clouds that scud overhead are ravening monsters

and scavengers pick the bones of the precious dead. There's always
        worse to fear. Ought I therefore pray
to arrive there, beyond fear, in the only safe
        place there is? It can't be far from Tomis.

I, 11

What you now hold in your hands, what you've been reading,
                                                    whoever
        you are, in whatever parlor, bedroom, or study,
I have been writing on decks, propped up against bulkheads,
        or on rough tables that inns offer, by lamps
that gutter, crazily ominous—as I am said to be
        myself. The roar of the sea, the yaw of the ship,
the spray aspersing the manuscript page in hand . . . Nothing
        has broken the trance in which I have persevered.
It's not a boast, for I haven't exerted myself except
        as a madman might as he holds onto something,
to anything at all, repeating his useless gesture
        beyond any meaning. The drowning are said to grasp
at any piece of flotsam. This has been my straw.
        What have I better to do when the rigging whines
and the helmsman shouts his curse at the wave bearing down on
                                                    him,
        indifferent and mighty as the gods themselves
seem? I keep out of their way. I write. It doesn't make
        any difference whether it's good or not,
and I have no idea any more, myself. The sailors,
        surviving the storm, will arrive at a safe harbor
which for me will be another kind of horror:
        ruffians, bandits, ambitious politicos, looking

to make points somewhere, and all of them out for my blood,
    while I scribble, scribble desperately on.
Look like a madman, and maybe the villains will leave me alone,
    finical as they are. And you, kind reader?
Hello? Are you there? If so, indulge these verses of mine.
    They don't come from my garden or that old couch
I used to sprawl on. Not that I put that wonderful comfort
    to such good use. My facility then was more
worthy of blame than my clumsiness seems now. And that's
    assuming readers, people paying attention.
You are conventional figures, Theorcritan shepherds and farmers,
    nearly real and always around to perform
necessary duties—such as fishing out
    from the slosh of surf a glittering bottle, sealed . . .
and, yes, look, with a message inside. You open it up
    to read the last cry from an old wreck.
Will you be the connoisseur of its style, or will your heart
    open itself in charity to pain's
plain speaking? Reader, whoever you be, I trust you
    to wish me well a little, to hope the storm
abated after all and the sun shone down
    upon this completed page its first wan ray.

Book II

What am I doing, still writing these books? The labor
    is great and there's no profit in it, to me
or anyone else. I'm digging my own grave, my talent
    an indifferent spade. Just as indifferent, the Muses
were never my friends. Paramours, more like. Demimondaines,
    out for themselves and a good time. Surprised?
I shouldn't be. The lesson is ancient. Popular, famous,
    I was a public plaything; the public wearies,
casts its toys away, like a bored child, picks up
    a new bauble. But Caesar's briefest frown
has its lasting effect. My *Art of Love* was not
    well liked. "Begone!" he said, and it was,
and I along with it. I should ape my master,
    echo his "Begone!" and let the Art
take itself away. The Muses with it, those tramps . . .
    But whom else do I turn to, lonely, cold,
and dying of thirst for the liquid flow of good talk
    and laughter? It's crazy to laugh all by yourself.
But how else does the wounded gladiator return,
    after he's healed, to try the arena again?
A battered ship, repaired, refitted, sets out again
    on the dangerous sea; its timbers creak complaint.
So I address the mountain—and claim to be clearing my throat.
    Think of Telephus, wounded by the spear
of mad Achilles. The only cure was rust from that same
    spear. He had to go back, seek out Achilles,
and ask for his cure, his life . . . And how do you think he
    felt? I've no hope of a cure. Poems
can never do much more than embellish real power,
    music at a parade, or the colored bunting
beneath a flag. Caesar commissioned hymns to Apollo
    to be performed at the games—but no one supposed

the games were played to accompany the singing of hymns.
    Nevertheless, the program required, tradition
demanded, and good manners assumed a show of attention
    to the recitation of pious verses. And Caesar
may be in that habit, so I can assume a free-
    floating, distracted, partly imagining, partly
attentive mind, lulled as the god himself may be lulled
    by hymns, and as well disposed to grant favors.
Or pardon sins. If every crime, every error of man
    brought down the thunderbolt it deserved
from Jupiter, he'd have been cleaned out aeons ago.
    Mercy is economical—for gods
and emperors too, their agents, in whom that same indulgence
    is right and fitting, whether by calculation
or a generous impluse, perhaps divinely inspired.
    So you have pardoned conquered foes, not only
sparing their lives but putting them to your own use,
    investing in them riches and honors to yield
as so many fertile fields increase to what you have planted.
    And I? Who have never taken arms against you?
Can I not plead my cause, looking at their worse cases,
    and offer myself, my heart that was always loyal.
(By earth and sea and sky, I swear this is the truth!)
    I can't imagine what is the sense in making
me an example, or in keeping me out here in exile.
    Back in Rome when crowds in the forum prayed
for your long life, that you might make your way
    late to the stars of heaven, wasn't my voice
mixed in with the others in chorus? And did I not offer
    incense in your behalf to further our prayer
for your sake, and the state's, and therefore for all our good?
    What threat can I pose, or what good can I be . . . ?
Innocuous as I am, I don't even make an example
    to warn others who might require warning

of what the results of disobedience must be.
  My books praise your name—those you dislike,
but the *Metamorphoses* too. Not that you need praise,
    but even Jupiter's pleased to be celebrated
and figure in the songs of men, the great chorus
    or the single voice, quavering. Caesar, I pray you,
listen, accept my tribute, as Jupiter also accepts
    as well as the blood of a hundred flawless bulls
the little sprig of incense offered up sincerely.
  I wonder who it was who did me that favor,
reading you my verses—and what could his motive have been?
    How was it he chanced upon those lines,
the playful, naughty bits rather than decorous others
    in which I do you honor? Was it malice?
Envy? Mischief? A grudge, left over from some affront
    I cannot remember? I conjure up the faces
I used to know searching for someone I might blame:
    my own face stares back at me, culprit ·
and victim. Disaster blurs such distinctions. In shock,
    I contemplate the rubble about me, dusty,
dazed. When a house collapses under its own weight,
    the fault—that first rift—may have been small,
nothing much to see. But then a creak, a low
    rumble, and . . . ruin, total ruin. So,
with me. The prudent crowd is right to have kept its distance,
    taking its cue from you. But I can remember
better times when your favor shone on me like a sun
    in whose light I grew and cast a shadow
larger than myself. I was your magistrate,
    deciding suits, acting as referee,
respected for my judgments. Now I'm the one judged,
    and virtues don't count. It's like a ship
at sea: one mistake, one terrible storm
    will send that seamanship, seaworthiness

down to the bottom, the men, the craft, the cargo lost.
　　Sunk, I waste my time wondering still
which particular wave was the one that did me in.
　　Whatever I saw, it was only through purest chance—
or mischance, I should say. As Actaeon might have said,
　　having beheld the goddess naked. (His hounds,
unimpressed by this plea, tore him apart alive.)
　　I am much better off, except that my hopes
nibble my toes or scamper and tickle my tenderest places
　　in an exquisite torture. I am not even *exiled*
but *relegated*. Today, tomorrow, perhaps the day after,
　　what news may arrive with that pardon I dream of,
and a summons home? Restored to the city of Rome, to life,
　　how can I fail to demonstrate your greatness?
Anybody can kill. The arena's wild beasts
　　can tear the heart out of a living creature.
Only a god can restore life to inert meat.
　　But such a miracle you can perform for me,
moribund as I am, here at the very edge
　　of the land of the living—and by the merest nod!
What you have already shown corrects my enthusiastic
　　Muse in a demonstration of restraint
impressive not only as justice or politics but as art.
　　You spoke against me, but not in the senate and not
in a session of special court. You kept it a private matter
　　as much as you could, for which my expression of thanks
sounds in every breath I draw and beats in my breast
　　with every thump of my heart. And my chagrin
for having displeased my lord who has shown me such kindness
　　is all the greater. Nature, the face of the gods,
rages, the seas and skies glower in storm but then
　　relent. I have seen a towering elm blasted
by a thunderbolt of the angry Jove—and then the tender
　　tendrils of vine that seemed to bind its wound.

Where there is such a healing, how can there not be hope?
    I remember, of course, your prohibition of hope—
but in the shimmer of heat even inert objects
    twitch into life. Out here, rehearsing the scene—
my only occupation, my passion, or say my craze—
    it wriggles in my emotion's fever, its truth
twisting: was it not mercy, another show of kindness
    that prompted you? If so, does it not follow
that your prohibition reverses itself, is grounds for hope?
    It's too intricate; I suspect it myself,
knowing how by such desperate cerebrated constructions
    the mind will try to wriggle free of distress.
As with the blowing winds, there is no constant madness
    but gusts, buffets, and then they subside, lulled
into a seemingly sane calm that never lasts.
    So my hopes subside into that same
abeyance or obedience, or, say, into acceptance,
    but from a new quarter begin again,
and once more I call out to you with their wild wail:
    By the gods above (and may they grant you long
years of life—as they must if they have any love for Rome)
    and by the fatherland (of which you are
the father of all the people of whom I have been one),
    I pray that you may receive from your grateful city
payment in full of the debt of love that each of us owes you
    for services received of word and deed
and spirit! May your household prosper, may Livia live
    in happy union—matchless match—with you!
I pray, too, for your son, Tiberius, that he,
    an old man with an older father, may rule.
And let me include your grandsons, Germanicus and Drusus,
    praying that their stars may keep the ascendance
in which they have begun, fortunate omens gracing
    the long and tranquil twilight of your life.

You raise a skeptical eyebrow, wonder if my well-wishing
    is under compulsion? Let me confess it is—
but what have I confessed? The father of all the gods
    compels by his power and majesty our prayers.
Where else shall we turn for help, relief, or for mercy?
    But remember, too, how I am a writer, my pen
the best part of me, truest witness, my soul's mirror.
    Words for me are as real as the world they describe.
Imagine how for the blind, a description, say of a room,
    becomes the room. You tell me there's a door
and my faith believes: I turn; I trust enough to move;
    I hold forth my hand to feel the air
confirm the truth of what you have told me, inch by inch,
    to which I owe my life, moment by moment.
Constrained or not, my prayers on you behalf are sincere,
    authentic as anyone's anywhere in the world.
Can you not find it within you to take some satisfaction
    of the kind you might take, pausing before a mirror,
some self-recognition in the words I'm offering up?
    In exchange for which, I ask only your mercy
this far—that I may have reason yet to hope,
    to keep alive some glimmer of expectation
of moderation. You needn't bring me all the way home,
    but grant me only a milder and a nearer
place of relegation. Let me sing your praises
    somewhere a little less remote than this,
in a place where the accent of Latin accommodates to the ear
    with a natural grace and ease. Is that too much?
There have been other offenders, other exiles sent
    away from the gates of Rome—but no one farther
than I've been sent. Was I the worst man in Rome,
    deserving this extremity? The fog
rises out of the ground and freezes into wraiths
    that lurk, bizarre and frightening, beyond

the laws of Rome. The brink of the world is here! A day's
    walk from here—or even half a day's—
and one has crossed the line into barbarian country,
    savage lands where wild beasts roam in packs,
and wilder men . . . as men will be without the restraints
    of customs, piety, of civilization,
which is what we are and what the two of us are about.
    I do not mean to presume. I remember, Caesar,
vividly, my offenses, both my crime and my blunder,
    and diffidently I advert to those delicate subjects,
or anyway to the one, the matter of public record,
    my literary offense—my dirty book.
Not that I wish to open old wounds that have healed,
    but let me, like a gentle doctor, probe
to confirm the diagnosis. Even among divine
    minds, error is possible. In the press
of weightier business, even the great father, Jove,
    may miss a trifle. And I'd be mad to suppose
that in the concerns of the world's chief executive officer
    and first citizen, my unequal measures,
these elegiac lines, would somehow float to the top
    of the piles of papers—writs, contracts, edicts,
petitions, charters, and treaties—arranged upon your desk.
    For you to have devoted any time
yourself to reading my little salon diversions is not
    probable. Suppose, instead, some earnest
youngster, inexperienced, eager to please. I'd guess
    the report would not have been made by a very senior
aide but by his assistant's deputy's clerk's trainee,
    and then passed upwards, and at each step endorsed
by a new set of initials, progressively more impressive
    if less atentive. Allow me to cite a passage
someone overlooked that speaks to the point directly:
    "Abjuring the matron's modest robes and ruffles,

I sing of licit love, the chase after fair game,
    and celebrate lovers rather than libertines."
What could be clearer than that? And what could be less improper?
    It isn't, I can imagine you thinking, enough.
The words of poets weasel; the lawmaker's ideal
    is clarity, is it not, and straightforwardness.
Why can't poets write that way, a word, a phrase,
    or a sentence meaning one thing only, this
and not that, the one as distinct from the other? But no,
    irony seduces and paradox
winks, inveigles, writhes, refuses to be pinned down.
    A man of letters is not a man of his word.
Do I have them right, the objections that first arise in your mind?
    Perhaps I should make them stronger, less abstract,
more pointed: for instance, your doubts about my disclaimer
    as a disingenuous ruse, a flimsy pretext.
How, you ask, can I know whether wives and matrons will not
    read and put to use my poem's suggestions,
even if that might pervert (along, no doubt, with much else)
    the poem's intention? The parenthetical phrase
I assign you condescends to the same ironic twist
    and turn, but let me reply in unadorned
and straightforward language, appropriate for discussion
    of serious questions affecting the common weal.
The question is whether wives ought ever to be allowed
    to read at all. Women likely to err
will find in whatever poem they happen to glance over
    inspiration, permission, even instruction
for wrongdoing. Ennius, high-minded Lucretius,
    or any of those bards, however revered,
will offer rude suggestions to people on the alert.
    There isn't a single literary work
without its risk to the soul to which it presumes to speak,
    but that doesn't mean poetry ought to be banned.

Anything useful to man or woman entails some risk.
    Fire, for instance, is necessary, is vital,
distinguishes us from beasts who stand in the shivering cold,
    helpless. It is civilization's emblem,
but accidents happen and crime is not altogether unknown—
    arson, I mean. Or better, think of the uses
of all those herbs and powders physicians carry around,
    cures in the right dosage but dangerous too:
in the wrong hands they're poisons. Or think of a short sword—
    a bandit's weapon or honest man's defense
against that same bandit. So it is with verse,
    which in the honest minds of decent people,
men or women, single or married, young or old,
    is an innocent pleasure, altogether harmless,
even mine. Suppose, if you will, that among the crowds
    in the seats of the coliseum a woman glances
left, then right, then behind her, and sees some appealing man,
    a stranger, perhaps . . . Or, no, someone she knows,
has arranged to meet this way, converting the public occasion,
    exploiting it, perverting it. Suppose
such a thing can happen, assume that it sometimes does,
    will you close down the games, prohibit the circus?
Or let us change the setting, staging the same action
    on the portico of one of the sacred temples.
Are the temples in that event all to be closed down?
    It's not so far-fetched, for the truly determined
woman could claim the risqué suggestion came from the god's
    example as she looked up and saw the clouds
and thought of Jupiter's lust for Danaë and the rain.
    The other gods and goddesses conspire,
as concupiscent as he, offering lewd examples
    just as beguiling, just as naughty to her
who looks to them for permission or reads in their bad behavior
    a natural law compared to which our morals

are vainglory, presumption, vanity, arrogance, pride—
    worse offenses than sexual indiscretion.
Juno, Venus, Mars, Isis, Luna, Ceres . . .
    the wife who is tottering near the edge, dizzy,
and about to fall will feel the sweet vertiginous tug
    of all their stories. The guilty eye will see
in the perfectly innocent glass her own soul's reflection,
    just as the honest wife, like the innocent maiden,
will escape, untouched, by whatever corruption she chances upon.
    Still, I do not deny my authorship.
I welcomed the credit and must, in fairness, accept the blame
    for my tastes, my talent, my Muse: *The Art of Love*
was just what its title said it was, nor do I attempt
    to disavow it. Mine is the error and fault.
I could have sung about Troy or the seven against Thebes,
    picked from the noble, conventional, and safe
subjects something suitably pious, something uplifting.
    Your own heroic deeds offer a subject
to challenge and stimulate the talents of any poet—
    but I couldn't see how lucky I was to live
in Rome in your time. I suppose my eyes were dazzled,
    or perhaps I knew my limits. A little talent
quails before a subject of too great an importance.
    As the weekend sailor of one of those little skiffs
avoids the open water and worries about the winds
    when the bay or pond he likes to sail gets choppy,
knowing his limitations and those of his craft, I too
    held to the shallows and kept my cargoes light.
I admit at once what the world has always been able to see—
    that I am a trivial person, sometimes amusing,
entertaining I hope, but hardly a serious bard.
    If I hadn't been blessed or cursed with a little talent,
nobody would have noticed my personal shortcomings.
    There are lots of men and women in Rome today

just as frivolous. Lucky or shrewd, they don't write.
    Wisdom and talent don't always coincide,
and I have had to work with whatever the gods gave me.
    It never crossed my mind that that knack I have,
left to its own devices, could be a source of danger
    to me and a possible nuisance to Rome or to you.
Clever, but not smart, I simply couldn't see it.
    Now I wonder why I ever began,
or why my doting parents indulged their adorable child
    setting me loose among the glories of letters.
Why did I learn to read? What good has it done me?
    Beguiling, yes, but treacherous—like the water
at a seaside resort where every summer some clumsy fool
    venturing out too far, going too deep,
not understanding how he can barely paddle around,
    gets caught, panics, drowns. And days later
the body washes ashore, and mothers warn their children
    who, for a week or two, mind and are careful.
Still, if I have annoyed, I've done no serious harm,
    have taught nobody's wife how to deceive
her husband . . . How could I, being myself transparent
    and an incompetent liar? Not that a poet
must have the same morals, good or bad, as his verse.
    My Muse is raffish perhaps, but not I.
Virgil wasn't a farmer. Terence didn't carouse.
    My poems don't corrupt, aren't wicked,
and I'm even less corrupting or wicked than any of them.
    Besides, if you look at the classics, every poet
writes of love. The readers expect it, even demand it.
    Anacreon writes of venery and wine;
Sappho, whom all the ladies read, teaches of love.
    Callimachus confesses to wanton delights
of illicit love. Will you exile them, or will you ban
    their books? Or the plays of Menander boys and girls

study in school? Love, and again and again, love!
    Even Homer is one long tale of love,
its complications, its terrible consequences—Helen's
    adultery causes the war and Agamemnon's
adultery starts the quarrel between himself and Achilles.
    And what is the *Odyssey's* story but that of a wife's
ten-year temptation, her wavering faith, her last-
    minute reprieve? And all that time, her husband,
Odysseus, is occupied how with Circe and with Calypso,
    goddesses both? But Homer is not forbidden.
The most solemn, the almost sacred kind of writing
    where art and philosophy meet at religion's borders,
is tragedy—which deals with love and its disorders.
    Think of *Hippolytus:* Phaedra, the stepmother, loves
her husband's son. Or think of *Aeolus,* where there is passion
    of sister for brother. The list can go on and on.
Medea, the Oedipus cycle, *Agamemnon, Electra* . . .
    I'm not just showing off how much I remember
without my books, how well my memory still supplies me
    with all the resonant names—although I cling
with particular fervor to what I have managed to keep and mourn
    bitterly the names and the lines that have faded
away, wracking my brain to retrieve whatever I can.
    The point is the general truth that poets sing
always of love and death, how one answers the other,
    how each implies and even demands the other.
Beginnings and endings, they both speak to us of our lives
    and what a life can be in value, in meaning,
to what extent it is touched and changed by the gods' attentions.
    Is it better or is it worse to be ignored?
We ask the question as if we had the power to choose,
    but recognize that we all have those two moments,
at our beginnings and then at the moment we face our ends,
    when each of us is in the hands of the gods

where the tragic hero lives, suffers, and dies in that blaze
　　of continuous meaning we both crave and fear.
Children are curious, want to collect the lurid details
　　of sex and of death as well; poets are more
concerned with their possible meanings—what life itself suggests
　　when love goes wrong and lovers lie down alone
in death's tight embrace. How could it happen so?
　　What kind of world, what kind of life is this?
Those are the obvious questions to which our finest minds
　　are always drawn, while the rest of us wish them well,
eager for answers. Writers of coarse tales poke fun
　　not at the subject but our obsession with it,
our helplessness before it. Eubius, Aristides,
　　and Hemitheon wrote their comic-erotic stories,
I do believe, to protest the fascination we all
　　share but refuse to admit to one another.
I hardly need defend against the possible charge
　　that what I'm saying applies only to Greek
but not to Roman writers, that they're corrupt and depraved
　　while we're steadfast in virtue. It isn't so.
The human condition doesn't change. The *civis Romanus*
　　is not a new and different order of man,
but the same old item, luckier, better governed,
　　a little more powerful, but begotten
the same old way. And we die just like anyone else.
　　The same old teasers perplex us, embarrass,
seeming so rich in answers but never yielding them up.
　　Ennius therefore speaks of love, and Lucretius
describes the causes and consequences of passion's fire.
　　Catullus writes of himself, daring to throw
the torchlight of attention on his most private moments,
　　to get to the truth of the matter as he knew it
best. There were risks of course, for his own reputation
　　as well as the moral tone of Rome—and he took them

rightly and uprightly. Calvus is just the same.
    Both of them changed the names of their paramours,
but everyone found a guide to tell who the real people
        were, which is why in Ticidas' verse or Memmius'
or that of Cinna or Anser, or Cato, or Cornificius,
        or Varo of Atax there's almost a contest of candor
where each tries to confess more of his personal life
        to shock, to ingratiate, to enlist the readers'
feelings of sympathy, of intimate understanding.
        Or think of Hortensius' work, or Servius' poems,
or Sisenna's (does anyone still read him?). Consider Gallus,
        whose difficulties were never written but oral:
the influx of too much wine, the efflux of too much boasting.
        But best of all, I appeal on the grounds of Tibullus
and what he was able to publish. In the name of fairness and

                                                              reason,
        if what he did was permitted, I can't understand
how what I have done should be cause for any objection.
        Tibullus goes way beyond the art of love
or even the tricks of seduction (for which I am mouldering here),
        and arrives, by a kind of morbid fascination,
at the moral depths, the bottom. He addresses the liar's craft.
        Remember how his faithless Delia treats him,
making the same denials, swearing the same false
        oaths to him as he has taught her to use.
He cannot, of course, believe her, but neither can he blame her
        for being such an apt pupil. He rages,
excoriates himself, believing himself to deserve
        such right and appropriate punishment, telling
the long list of his sins, his petty criminal's wiles.
        Yes, there's regret and even chagrin. The moral's
clear enough that a low life will bring a man down.
        But there the tricks are, for the eager youth,
the bored housewife, the restless matron to think about
        and perhaps to use if the need should ever arise.

I've never gone so far as to say which kinds of lotions
    will hide hickeys. Nowhere in my work
do I recommend making friends with the dog so it won't bark
    while you stand outside the house, waiting, watching
for the husband to leave and the wife to give the all-clear signal.
    I never talked about ways to prevent sneezes
that give you and the game away while you hide in the closet.
    I don't condemn Tibullus for this. The point
is that nobody else does either. His work is read and approved,
    as is that of Sextus Propertius. Those two,
with so much else in common, were models for me, masters,
    examples to follow, and now my justification.
I could adduce as well the names of living poets,
    some of them famous, others less so, all
qualified by their interest in love and its permutations,
    but I shouldn't want to put a colleague at risk—
even if I supposed I might then have a new neighbor.
    Besides, there's the contrary risk, that I could offend
by leaving somebody out who fancies himself as raffish,
    as ribald as the next man, as depraved . . .
You wouldn't want to turn us into a bunch of martyrs
    for individual freedom of expression
or whatever else, bestowing the wrong kind of glamor
    on poets and men of letters, turning us into
gladiators or charioteers who flirt with disaster
    and thereby fascinate a vulgar public.
It isn't a threat (out here, I'm not in any position
    to make plausible threats) but a speculation,
a vision of what could happen that neither of us would want.
    I return to the question. Let us consider whether
there's ever any effect of literature on life.
    Did any of those clever didactic poems
on playing with dice increase the number of games of chance
    played in Rome, or even the size of the bets?

I'd bet not. The point was to parody Hesiod's *Works*
    and Days and perhaps Virgil's adaptation.
Did the *Georgics,* for that matter, persuade many city dwellers
    to trade their urban careers for the satisfactions
that only farmers know? Nothing good or bad
    comes from reading a poem except the poem.
Even the masques where actors and actresses declaim,
    rolling their eyes, making their moves and moues
better suited to *salles privées* or bedrooms are harmless,
    provoking laughter as much as lust. We squirm
even as we applaud to see the husband outwitted
    once again. And the praetor approves and permits
those writers and actors a freedom I should imagine poets
    also deserve. It isn't fair or just
or reasonable. I think of nothing else, approach
    madness trying to puzzle it out, would rather
understand a principle, see the logic, and know
    my fault than be the victim of mere whim.
I try, therefore, to construct in my own mind your logic
    and compare my worst work to the public standard,
but cannot find the offense. I simply cannot see it!
    It must, I suppose, be there, somewhere, somehow . . .
But, sir, it was years ago. I don't still write that way.
    My concerns have changed; my style is different now.
The *Metamorphoses* and then the calendar poem,
    The Fasti, were inspiring and uplifting—
so I can't even reform, becoming that chastened, changed,
    and better man punishment ought to produce.
The change—I hope, the improvement—happened back in Rome
    years ago. Glance at the poems. Dip
at random into the scrolls and see with how much heart
    I sing of Rome's glories, my gratitude
and pride in being a Roman, and my great respect for you.
    I have already imposed on your time and attention

far too long. There are many more important matters
        awaiting your decision. Still, I appeal
to reason, to the enlightened rule of law, the ideal
        of fair treatment you represent to us all.
From eastern tyrants' whims there can never be an appeal—
        they can't afford to admit they've made mistakes
let alone correct them. Stronger, you can afford to review
        decisions that have been made perhaps too harshly.
I've never injured a soul! I've never insulted or libeled
        or ridiculed anyone. I, myself, am the only person
my feckless pen has ever damaged in any way.
        No Roman rejoices that I am exiled
or relegated here. Indeed, there are some who mourn.
        No one's rights in the case would be infringed
or interest overlooked if you were to show me mercy.
        I beg your indulgence—as any writer hopes
his reader will indulge him, will ignore the tangles of syntax,
        the limitations of style, the graceless moments,
and by a generous leap of the sympathetic heart
        arrive at the heart of my meaning. Would that I could
speak directly, throw myself on the ground before you,
        and let you hear my sobs as much as the words
strung upon them like beads upon a knotted string.
        My life is at your disposal. Father, protector,
I am a harmless beetle that's landed upon your sleeve.
        You have not crushed me but only flicked me away.
I lie on my back, helpless, awkward, and wriggle about
        begging the further favor that you right me.
It isn't even return to Italy that I ask,
        but somewhere civilized, where Latin is spoken,
safe enough for my wife to come to for a visit.
        I languish here. O Caesar, I offer thanks
for sparing my life and beg you only to be consistent;
        grant me as well a place and a way to live it.

Book III

III, 1

An exile's book, I come in fear here to the city.
  Hold your hand out, reader. Open your heart
to a poor pariah, a pilgrim. Do not recoil in fear
  or disgust. I promise, I won't infect you. Clean!
See? Look! Not a word about love or *The Joy of Sex*.
  I'm not joking. Or rather, my master isn't.
Surely, not about that, the work of his salad days,
  that ill-fated amusement. He hates it now.
Here you will see nothing but sadness, the lame lines
  of unequal couplets of elegy limping along,
footsore, heartsore. I come from far away to a city
  my master remembers from long ago. I greet you
looking much like a rustic, got up in the country manner
  because it is fitting so. Suppliant, beggar,
I cannot appear before you better groomed than my maker.
  My letters are blotted, words are crossed out, phrases
scratched in. There are blurs of tears and sweat. The Latin
  is shaky here and there, for I was composed
where no Latin is heard. Think of my maker singing,
  the only bird of his kind on a barren island
where gulls scream and wrangle of nothing but fish and hunger.
  A lark, he can warble more or less by instinct,
but cannot refine his performance by hearing kindred voices.
  Pity me, friend. Do me the kind service,
an act of piety really, and tell me where I should go,
  where a stranger just arrived in the city
might look for shelter. Tell me whatever you'd tell a tourist—
  that this is Caesar's forum, and over there
is the Via Sacra, and further along, the Temple of Vesta
  (the Palladium's inside and the sacred fire).
I've heard of these sights of course. My master can draw a map
  that would show them all, but the scale is amazing, awesome.

The Palatine Gate, right? And there is the Jupiter Stator,
    where Rome was first founded. And those doors
with the oak leaves and the laurel? Surely the home of a god!
    The decorations proclaim it a house of joy . . .
or perhaps they mark the peace its owner brings to the world,
    the evergreen of the laurel a sign of the glory
everlasting the house and its occupant both deserve.
    It's Caesar's house. The inscription over the door
declares that by the aid that comes from within these walls
    citizens of Rome have been saved. End quote.
Kindest of fathers, add one more name to the list
    of citizens you've saved. I think of my master
far from here, in exile, at the empire's very edge,
    whose punishment it is to imagine Rome
and remember every mile of billowing sea and hard
    rocky ground that separates there from here.
This is the shrine that marks the place where lightning struck.
    My paper ought to turn pale, my script shudder,
and the words on my pages twitch like stimulated nerves.
    The feet of my verse should tremble as I utter
the prayers my master groaned at the moment of my creation.
    I stand as if struck dumb and seem to stagger,
backing away. I try somehow to collect myself,
    as I recall my mission. I climb the steps
of Apollo's temple Augustus built on the Palatine.
    There, beyond the marble columns and statues,
a sanctuary beckons, the library Augustus
    established, open to any who would study
the wisdom of ages past and the present time. I come
    seeking my brothers (except of course that rogue
the dalliance of whose begetting our father so much regrets).
    When a stranger enters a town where relatives live,
he looks them up—perhaps for a hand-out, a meal, a bed,
    but most of all for the warmth of the blood tie.

The crowds of a city are cold. Loneliness blows like a wind
    with a sharp bite from off the empty fens.
A brother's embrace would be better than wine then, but I can't
    find them. I search, but the guards tell me to leave.
I don't understand. I've tried to be quiet. I haven't disturbed
    the scholars who sit at the tables. They hustle me out.
There's another temple I try, near the Octavian gate,
    but there I can't even get in. I go to a third,
the Temple of Liberty. There, they let me know the score—
    I'm banned. We all are banned, all Ovid's children.
The fate of the father dogs the heels of his offspring. Sir,
    I beg you, hear me! Or having shown me the kindness
thus far of your attention, and knowing I'm hardly a danger
    to Rome or the mighty Augustus, take me in.
In houses and hearts of the people, there must be places to hide
    till Caesar hears my prayers and one day relents.

III, 2

I don't feel guilty. If I did, I'd bear it better
    to be shut away here on this bleak shore.
It's worse this way. One could make epigrams about it:
    "His art was waggish but his life was sad."
I don't joke any more, have become the butt of jokes.
    The long uninterrupted gray of the sky
and sea is a huge joke. I used to sit by the fire
    or, when the weather was fine, stroll in the garden,
soft, incredibly pampered, and yet I have held up,
    survived one danger after another.
Thinner, toughened, tanned, I've managed to clench my teeth
    and hang on, get through the next hour,

the next day, to get to my destination, the fate
    Caesar decreed for me . . . And now I wonder
whatever for? For this, did I endure those perils?
    So many times have I knocked at my tomb's door,
but in vain. It did not open. And I am sitting here,
    with nothing left to hope for, nothing to fear,
nothing to do but face that empty gray expanse,
    and think back to those storms, the ships, the brigands
that could have done me the service and held open that door
    through which it could have been granted to me to pass,
escaping after all the limitless decree,
    leaden as that skyscape and seascape
hanging over me here. The joke is living through
    to the far side of terror, the ennui,
the pointlessness, where each breath I draw is a burden.
    Among the unanimous gods, I pray for one
to relent, dissent, and grant that door I've been knocking on
    may open so that at last I may come home.

III, 3

The hand is another's, yes, but the words are still mine.
    I dictate from a sick-bed. It's the water
I haven't got used to yet, or the food, the climate, the view . . .
    But I think it's the water that's got me, and I lie here
fevered, imagining crisp sheets and delicate broths
    on pretty trays. And the visits of kindly friends.
The comforts of being sick back home in Rome! My eyes
    brim with tears. I reach out to touch the rough
log wall and confirm that it's not merely a nightmare.
    This is real. The other's the dream. It's crazy.

Which is to say I begin to doubt my own five senses.
    I get things jumbled, forget what day it is,
forget where I am . . . A blessing, a momentary escape,
    except that every time I come back to myself
it's Tomis I come back to, the same bed in the same
    room in this poor hut. But when I wander
they tell me I say your name, that I make mumbling noises
    as if I'm talking. Talking to you I suppose.
Despite the distance then, you're still a help, a comfort,
    and if I survive (as now seems likely) I'll owe
a further debt to that phantom wife you have become.
    Believe in her, as I try to believe
in the phantom of myself who walks with you now in the garden,
    who attends you always, as I should like to do
in the simple flesh. Conceits are what we're driven to, all
    we have—but like some pastries, they are cloying,
and what seemed at first delicious turns abruptly revolting.
    It's better to admit the plain truth: grief
that you're there and that I'm here and will stay here.
    In my darkest moods, I wonder about dying
and whether even then Caesar will show me the mercy
    of letting my body be carried back to Rome
so that I might be laid to rest in my native earth.
    It doesn't matter much, but I think about it.
It's a way of avoiding the other more troublesome thoughts—
    of what a good death would be like, to weaken
in one's own room, in one's familiar bed, with friends,
    relatives, one's wife in attendance, weeping,
offering what comfort a moment like that allows.
    The easy passage, the chance to say farewell,
to offer a blessing, lament, and face the moment together.
    Out here, my eyes will just go blank
as my soul turns from the outer to inner and larger blankness.
    Death, here is a commonplace thing, vulgar,

all its formality gone, hardly worth remarking—
    which means that life is common and vulgar too.
I'm sorry to be depressing, can imagine you reading this,
    stretching forth your arms and calling my name.
Or maybe not. Probably not. Another conceit.
    For after that first and only separation,
none of these others matters. I'm no further away
    than I was before you opened this scroll to read
the same old complaints we both have learned to live with,
    and by, and even for. Nothing since then
matters—not even letters, not even one like this
    dejected complaint, can add much to your burden.
Our hearts, little by little, harden. It's sad, yes,
    but even to this sadness we learn to adapt.
I have been giving some thought to the problem of souls
                  and whether,
    after we die, they continue to flit about
in the empty air. I think Pythagoras says they do
    and stay wherever the person happened to die—
which is why certain places seem to be sacred (or haunted).
    A difficult doctrine, and very bleak, to imagine
my soul still here after I'm dead and buried,
    still in exile, still longing for Rome.
Can I suppose that the soul somehow follows the body
    so that, if my bones are shipped back in an urn,
the soul will follow along? Ought I to ask permission?
    But who would deny so small a thing as that?
Who would object? Would Caesar risk the appearance of spite?
    Would he turn your obedience to my wishes
into Antigone's noble and ruinous triumph? No,
    we can depend, I'm sure, upon his shrewdness.
I have composed an inscription suitable for my tomb,
    dignified but not altogether boring:
NASO AM I, THAT WIT WHO VERSES MADE,
ANOTHER INNOCENT BY LOVE BETRAYED.

I BEG YOU, LOVER, PRAY FOR ME (OR I
SHALL PRAY IT FOR YOU): "SOFT MAY HIS BONES LIE."
No censor will worry about it—or I won't worry
    whether one does or not. My books will remain
my only real monuments, better than any marble.
    So it doesn't matter, except that it pleases me
(and that, good wife, is all a poet should have to consider).
    I'd dictate more, but my voice is getting tired.
My throat is dry. I feel the fever coming on.
    My love, fare, as I do not here, well.

III, 4

I write to acknowledge a debt and even, in part, repay it,
    for I recall the hour of my ruin
and who was there to witness and speak the words of comfort
    (and who wasn't). I still remember your tears
and, wishing you well, I hope your griefs may always be such—
    generous empathy on the behalf of others,
that catastrophe keep its distance, that you be spared what I
    have suffered and still suffer. This extreme
is not wisdom, and yet there's a kind of authority in it.
    Or, if not, I beg you to listen, to heed
my well-intended words and the warning of my example.
    The message is simple, even obvious: Flee
fame! Shun the famous. The heights we all strive for
    are dangerous, and the risks just aren't worth it.
You look to powerful friends to protect you in times of trouble.
    but powerful friends can be the trouble. Private
men and women, out of the limelight, live, work,
    love, grow old, die, and are perfectly happy.

There's nothing wrong with that, but how we looked down our
noses
    at the poor provincials. They were right, and we
were wrong, stupid, crazy . . . Icarus flew high,
    and Daedalus didn't. We know what happened to them.
I'm punished here for offending the Emperor Augustus,
    but also for being stupid, for thinking glamor,
glitter, and glitz were important, were what my talent deserved.
    The truth pains me, I see it so clearly now.
Talent deserves quiet and time to grow and produce.
    What more could any poet want, my friend?
Humility, patience, circumspection, simplicity . . .
    they aren't abstract virtues but strategies,
ways of living, better, safer, more satisfying
    than the way I used to live in Rome. Learn,
profit from me and my woeful example! Reef your sails.
    Walk softly. Learn to enjoy the small
blessings of life, the things you take for granted and I
    dream about with envy. A simple supper
with a few friends (my eyes well up at the thought of it now)
    is better than any banquet I ever attended.
The day I left, you came to see me off, faithful
    as always. I remember your pained face—
you looked the way I felt. And even now, I hear
    you still defend the name of your banished friend.
I weep to hear it, tears of gratitude and affection.
    In love, I tell you: live unenvied. Flee
the high life. Cling to a few loyal friends like yourself.
    My heart is with you. Only my husk is here.
The skies above me are frosty. Even the stars here
    shrivel with cold. Beyond, there's the Bosporus,
the Don, the Scythian marshes, and then nothing but ice,
    empty uninhabited wastes, the world's
dizzying edges, vacant as death itself. I'm closer
    to that than to a fatherland, wife, and home.

My imagination fails, returns to its old haunts,
    and I see familiar places back in the city,
a comfort and a torment, as life itself must be
    to a man dying in pain. He holds on tight
to the pain as to life itself, as I do now to the image
    of that beloved face that appears before me.
My wife's gift of love is a burden and also a lesson
    in how to bear the burden. So I try.
And you, too, my friend, of whom I so often think,
    you keep me going. I fear to name you here.
Back in the old days, it would have been a gesture
    of honor, of friendship. Now, only disgrace
stands within my gift. I know the contagion I carry.
    Only upon the tablets of my heart
where there's no possible danger, do I dare write your name.
    Or read it—for you have written it with deeds
time can't dim and I remember with gratitude.
    You know who you are. A trick of fate
has landed me here, but now your fame has spread to the last
    bastion of Rome! It's not altogether a joke.
Kindness keeps on going, reverberating, a bell
    in the night's quiet hours. Blessings, friend.
I'm grateful for all your efforts, great and small, then
    and now. I hope you remember my advice.
If you do, you'll never sit, writing with frozen fingers
    long letters like this to friends in Rome.

III, 5

Ours was a minor friendship, easy enough to forget
    or deny if you'd chosen to, an acquaintance really

that both of us always meant to pursue, but Rome is busy.
    A party's promptings are gone by the next noon,
and the months melt away like sherbets. You and I
    would have kept on with kindly but vague intentions
of getting together soon. But at my ruin, when all
    fled in fear of contagion, cutting their closer
longer ties, you didn't. You came to touch the fallen
    body and prod it to see if the lightning bolt
had killed or only stunned me. You were not afraid
    to cross my threshold, give what all but two
or three of my oldest friends couldn't, tears, a pale
    wordless pity, your arms about my neck.
Brave and generous spirit, still loyal in my long
    absence, you know how *caro amico* stands
here in my text and life for the proper noun of your name.
    I keep in my heart's strongbox my real treasures—
a map of Rome and a few exemplary portraits, yours
    prominent among them. May gods grant
you strength to defend those toward whom your affection flows,
    and may mine be the closest disaster you ever know.
And if you were to ask, as you would, of course, how
    in my ruin I manage here on this distant shore,
I'd tell you the truth: it's only hope that keeps me going,
    a long slender thread that stretches from here
all the way back to Rome. If I twitch it right,
    deftly, lightly enough, and with luck, the somber
face of the god may lighten, may break into a smile.
    Speak for me, friend. You may be that thread!
Proclaim how a man's heart is the true measure of greatness,
    how noble spirits can gentle, how the lion
walks away when his foe is down, helpless before him.
    It's the mean wolf and the bear who don't relent,
delight in the bloody wallow and grin with the beastly gore
    shining upon them. We are not those beasts.

Who on either side at Troy was brave as Achilles,
    but at Priam's tears, was he not moved to pity?
Alexander the Great was also merciful. Think
    of how he might have had Porus killed but didn't,
and moved by his desperate show of pride, restored his throne;
    or how at Darius the Third's death, he gave
his own mantle to cover and honor his foe's corpse.
    The mighty can relent, and the most mighty
are the most likely and able. I think of nothing else,
    and don't believe I delude myself. Consider:
I never threatened Caesar's life (the life of the world),
    betrayed no secret, spoke nothing seditious . . .
My worst crime was to blunder onto the scene of a crime,
    but in all this time, mute, I ought to have earned
a little trust, I'd imagine. I do have grounds for hope,
    reasons that you might urge with a well-placed word.
Every day at sunrise, I wonder whether today
    the news will arrive at last that he has lightened
his harsh sentence, recast it to let me follow a little
    the light as it brightens, westering toward home.

III, 6

Old friend, good friend—the two of us go back a long way.
    You've never hidden it, couldn't, wouldn't want to.
No one in all of Rome meant more to me than you,
    and no one was closer to you than I. We were
a famous pair and famous as a pair, our friendship
    better known than either of us alone.
That you are open hearted and loyal to your friends, the gods
    know—or that particular god you love

knows very well. You've never had a secret you didn't
    confide in me, as I shared mine with you,
or all but one. I never told you what caused my ruin.
    Perhaps, if I had, you could have given advice
which might have kept me safe and I might still be back there
    living the old life. A mistake? Or fate?
Whatever I did was wrong, and what I might have done
    would also have turned out badly or even worse.
It's one of those dreams. One keeps on hearing the closing
                            of doors
    one never tried, thinking them all locked.
There's nothing left to do now but call out through them:
    remember me. Remember how we were,
and do what you can. You still must have some influence,
    couldn't have lost your charm or its dark twin,
the shrewdness that knows where and when and with whom to
                           use it.

    Do what you can for you old friend to assuage
the awesome god's anger, that it may relent a little
    and I be cast out not so far as I've been,
not to this uttermost, where no man utters words
    I think in during the day, dream in at night.
I won't go into the details for your safety's sake
    and my own sanity's, too. My mind refuses
to consider that time again: it's like a bloody wound
    I can't bear to look at under the bandage.
Even to touch that tender place brings a twinge of shame
    like physical pain. I sinned, but by my sin
sought no reward, advantage, gain . . . A folly, really!
    If I lie, do what you can to move my exile
even further away, for Tomis then would be
    too close to Rome, too cozy for such a shit.

III, 7

Go quickly, quickly written letter, to greet
    Perilla, my stepdaughter, leaping over
the wastes and waves as once our affections leapt
    over the obstacles shrewdness might have predicted
but could not charm away. Stepfathers try to be decent,
    neither indifferent nor yet over attentive,
and stepdaughters avoid comparing their late fathers
    with the new men their mothers have set up
as alien gods in the household's inner temple. They fail
    almost always. But somehow she and I
were blessed, came to be friends, her talent for living as great
    as her talent for making the verses I used to read.
I was her teacher, critic, her confidant and friend,
    and when you arrive, I expect she'll be with her mother,
posed as they often are together. Or she may be
    alone with the books she loves. But either way,
she'll welcome you right away, asking after my welfare.
    Tell her I live as I do not wish to live
and let her know I've returned to the Muses for whom I suffer,
    informing my thoughts and words with elegy's measure.
Ask her whether she still makes verses the way I taught her,
    or better than I taught—for my example
would not be apt to encourage even another Sappho.
    I used to read her admirable poems . . .
She may have given it up, but tell her to persevere
    and work her talent, if only she keeps away,
as anyone clever would, from didactic poems on Love.
    Let her not feel any chilling effect
of these cold winds nor suffer the burden of my exile.
    Speak to her. Tell her, "Keep at it, my girl.
Return to a noble art; offer your effort's tribute.
    Your beauty will fade, that smooth face show lines

the years will etch and then engrave deeper and deeper
    upon your remarkable brow. The treasures of youth,
time, that stealthy thief, will come to pilfer, and you
    will no doubt hear some day somebody saying,
'She was gorgeous once,' and stare into your glass
    and, full of grief, agree. Now you have money,
but think how Fortune's caprice can beggar even a Croesus.
    Of what you have and even of what you are,
know that nothing remains, that even the physical world
    shimmers, changes, one dream giving way
in the restlessness of the world's sleep to another and worse
    dream. It's only the blessings of heart and mind
that ever endure. In those you should put your trust."
    I offer my own example. You know how much
I lost when I was sent away into exile. Ruined!
    But see what I still have, my mind, my work.
Unless he put me to death, not even Caesar can take
    this from me or banish me from this.
And even then, the work would keep alive the best
    of what I am to survive at home in the minds
of those who love the art. Think how the grave yawns
    and gobbles everything else. Save what you can.

III, 8

The slow scud of the heavy clouds across a low
    sky is tempting, hypnotizing: the fancy
follows: there ought to be a way to harness and ride
    Triptolemus' car, or bridle the brace of dragons
Medea drove when she fled from Corinth. Oh, for the wings
    of Perseus or Daedalus to beat

the air thick as cream to float upon like those
    effortless clouds, light, lofty, aloof,
back to Roman skies! I'd gaze down to spot
    my house, pick out the figures of my friends,
and watch my wife look up, amazed to see me hover
    overhead like a huge gangly bird . . .
More like a huge fool. These are the prayers of a child,
    rehearsals of old myths, dreams, and lies,
as if the bitter truth were not bizarre enough.
    Augustus, the god, moved a hand and I
was gone, wafted away to the end of the known world.
    His is the power to put me in wingèd shoes,
to supply me with a flying chariot or to pucker
    his lips and blow a wind that will bear me up
like a feathered creature and set me down again wherever
    he pleases. It is to him I ought to address
an elegantly framed, measured, and artful prayer—
    or offer my bargain, which is what a prayer becomes
kept too long in the heart where it starts to turn and curdle:
    If not Rome, then anywhere but here
where the climate is foul, the air dank, the water rank,
    and the land barren and wild. I can't sleep.
Depression saps my strength, and my body's own weakness
    depresses whatever wan cheer I manage
at moments to muster. I can't eat: I'm losing weight
    and my color is awful. Here, in this faraway waste,
I waste away. I can look in the glass and see my fate
    looming as I dwindle, or turn around
and through the window observe a parade of nightmare creatures,
    barbarous and outlandish in dress and language,
that haunt my waking hours. Among them, even death
    must seem benign and welcome. I have the power
to summon him to lighten the harsh decree of Caesar . . .
    Why didn't he have me killed in Rome?

Was mercy in his heart? To that, then, I appeal:
    let it move Caesar to move me hence.

III, 9

Even here among inhumanly grunted place-names
    are (would you believe?) Greek cities. This
huddle of hovels was founded by colonists from Miletus
    who set up a trading post. It was they who named it
Tomis, in recognition (one cannot call it honor)
    of what had taken place and marked the place
in earlier days. It was off this very shore that the Argo
    hove to with Medea, Jason, and all
those Argonauts in flight from Medea's angry father,
    Aeëtes, the king of Colchis. You remember
the picturesque story? From those hills, the lookout
    spied the pursuing ship with familiar sails
and rang or blew or shouted the alarm. They swarmed aboard
    the vessel to haul away at the anchor cable
and the sheets and braces, desperate, watching Aeëtes' vessel
    bearing down, knowing it was hopeless . . .
But you don't just wait for disaster to overtake you.
    You do what you're trained to do or what your nature
allows you to do. For Medea, there simply weren't limits.
    It was all her fault. It was she who had dared,
and would again, the unspeakable, all but unthinkable act.
    She had to delay her father to save her lover
as well as his companions—not to mention herself.
    She turned to her brother Absyrtus, whom the king
had first sent in pursuit but who was now her captive.

How could she put him to use, to buy time
and distance from her father? She commandeered a sword
    and stabbed him in the side, and again, and again,
hacked him to bits, scattered the bloody pieces, and made
    a gory treasure hunt for King Aeëtes
who had to search for each piece and bury them all,
    as the Argo sailed away. This place, they call
Tomis—from *temno*, "to cut"—for him who was butchered here.

III, 10

I may be gone but the name of Naso perhaps still haunts
    the city, may yet be pronounced now and again.
Let those in whose generous thoughts it keeps a *pied à terre*
    know how I fare beneath the frozen glint
of stars that stud the sky above this forsaken shore.
    Around me cruel Sauromatians vie
with Bessi and Getae: the three tribes that have to share
    the woeful distinction of being the worst on earth.
In summer the river provides us a certain degree of protection,
    but summer is short. The winds blow from the north;
the fens freeze hard; and those desperate tribes can march
    over the ice and squeaky snow to plunder
whenever their mood or hunger prompts, which is all the time.
    The snow is nothing like what you have in Rome,
but constant. It falls and lies there under a wan sun
    and an impotent rain that cannot melt it but freezes
to make another crust for a new snowfall to cover
    deeper than before. The natives here
wrap themselves from head to toe in animal skins
    that show only a handsbreadth of face,

the brows and whiskers spangled with the glitter of hoarfrost.
    I've stopped for a drink and hardly even remarked
as the inkeeper peeled away the wineskin to leave the wine
    standing, frozen, in what was the wineskin's shape.
He hacked me a chunk of wine to drink or, rather, suck on
    as it thawed in my mouth. They mine water here,
dig it and lug it from ponds or the river that rings with hoof-beats,
    and it's a precious metal. Back in Rome,
one hears of a river freezing, but here even the sea
    turns solid. The harbor where ships rode
can bear a man, a horse, a team of oxen, their cart,
    loaded. I have walked out myself
to stand in mid-channel. If only Leander had waited,
    he wouldn't have had to swin the Hellespont,
but might have crossed here, on foot, with the fish below
    bumping their noses in vain as they lunged upwards
at the unattainable morsel, visible through the ice.
    That same ice invites the predatory
tribes from the northern wastes, scarecrows on gaunt horses
    who cross the empty landscape with empty bellies
and quivers full, and their eyes full of envy and hate.
    Careless of their own worthless lives,
they are therefore pitiless, savage, more like beasts than men,
    and awesome fighters. Our peasants flee before them,
saving whatever they've loaded onto their creaking carts—
    what's left behind is lost, burned, or butchered.
Worse, the plundering hordes shoot with poison arrows,
    picking off among the laggard farmers
one or another to fall in agony, stricken, dying
    as the venom spreads. But worst of all are the captives,
women mostly, the raiders' whim has chosen as slaves.
    They lead them away into exile, bound, weeping,
gazing behind as they're dragged out to the empty steppes
    for a last burning glimpse of their lives' ruin.

That awful vision they'll keep for the rest of their lives, a torment
    and yet a kind of comfort. They'll close their eyes
and that graven scene will glow, shimmering in the darkness
    for a terrible instant over and over again.
The landscape itself retains a look of reciprocal grief
    I'm not imagining. Countryside can show
cultivation, prosperity, a settled appearance
    that only years of peace provides where a man
can plant groves to yield a living to his grandchildren.
    Not here. The style is the quick foray.
The farmer raids the land as he himself is raided.
    He plows—if he plows at all—stopping to listen
and look to the left and right and over his shoulder for signs
    of marauders' movement. Abandoned fields witness
how the enemy's threat always and everywhere
    impends, is itself another enemy. Fear
is the weed that chokes the crops, blights the vines, sours
    the frothy must in the vats. Barbarian plants
invade the settled patches of cultivation as nature
    mimics the politics of the place. There are no
orchards here or fruits. Instead, the ground grows stones
    to fling as you flee, or break the teeth of your plow,
or break your heart unless it harden into a stone.
    Wretched, thus, I live in the land of wretches.

III, 11

You son of a bitch, nursed on dog milk and thirsting
    now for blood, you laugh at my misfortunes
and rail against me still! How can you be so cruel?
    What kind of flinty-hearted bastard are you?

Even in savage nature, there is a kind of mercy:
      storms abate; the appetite is sated
of fiercest beasts who retire to sleep and digest. What else
      can you want of me? What satisfaction is there
you can't already take in my misery? What more
      would you have them inflict upon me to amuse you?
I am oppressed by skies in which all constellations
      bode ill, while below the chill winds swirl,
remorseless as brutes who raid from the borders they roam,
                                      making
      gutteral cries that pass for human speech.
We are the sheep; the legion tries to be our shepherd;
      but those tribes are the beasts preying upon us.
At night, the ululation of wolves sounds in our ears,
      and I am roused from the torment of my dreams
of my wife, friends, and city. Would it not be enough
      that I feel the wrath of Caesar, Lord of the world?
Shouldn't that be sufficient, even for someone like you
      who delights in pain? Add to that these other
petty details of my life, the map of my wounds your rough
      tongue excoriates to bleeding again,
stung by your acid spittle . . . You deserve congratulations,
      eloquent in a cause already decided,
victorious in a contest in which the opposing party
      was vanquished from the start. The risk was small,
but don't let that diminish your feeling of having triumphed
      over my shadow. Desecrators of tombs
must have a like sense of achievement knocking down
      the monuments of heroes. Hector, alive,
fought his war, but dead and hitched to the Greek horses
      to be dragged in the dust, was no longer Hector
but only a piece of carrion. By that same token, I—
      or the Naso you knew in Rome—no longer exist.
Nothing remains but a wraith, an insubstantial phantom
      hardly worth attention, let alone rancor.

Why should you attack a ghost with intemperate, bitter
    words? Leave me alone—or the little that's left
of what I was. Even the heart of a hangman, hardened
    by his awful job, would melt at my sad case,
but you are a stern judge who wants to increase the sentence,
    making it longer and harder. But think of Busiris,
the wicked Egyptian king who offered foreigners up
    on the sacrificial altar—until the day
Hercules threw off his bonds and turned the tables,
    putting the king's eldest son on the altar
to suffer the brazen knife. Or think of that Sicilian
    tyrant for whom Perillus made his clever
toy, the metal bull inside of which a man
    could be roasted alive over a slow fire:
the bellows of pain echoed, resembling those of a bull.
    Delighted, shocked, Phalaris gave the order
that Perillus be the first to demonstrate the machine's
    verisimilitude. For ten years
Phalaris thus amused himself until his subjects,
    revolted, revolted, putting him in his place—
in the bull where he belonged. And you, my faithful tormentor,
    you who slake your thirst with my heart's blood,
who laugh at my woes and sit by your hearth imagining me
    freezing my ass out here in Tomis, you
deserve no less than those monsters got in the end.
    I warn you to keep your clumsy hands away
from my delicate wounds, allowing time to show me its mercy.
    Let the scar grow over the tender place,
for fate has its twists sometimes, its sudden violent reversals.
    For my crime—or mistake—I have been punished;
but yours, your obsessive interest in my wretched condition,
    your utter lack of charity, your gloating
could find for themselves one day some fitting chastisement.
    Forget my exile. Caesar's anger itself

is the torment I bear. That you may one day understand this
    is, believe me sir, my fervent prayer.

III, 12

The wind is out of the west again to inspire the frozen
    Pontus and bring the rigid corpse of the land
to life again. The bleak fields of brown stubble
    show a little green in the fresh shoots.
The slate gray of the sky relents to a shade not far
    from a real blue. There's a hint behind the morning
haze of a sun that may yet burn through a fair day
    when boys and girls will run through meadows to gather
wildflowers, and birds will chatter or even sing
    as anywhere else in the world. Somewhere, I guess
vines are coming to bud. (There are no vines around here.)
    Somewhere trees are sprouting those tiny leaves.
(There are no trees around here.) But the air is a little milder;
    one can breathe without feeling the daggers
of cold attacking one's breast, or even think of home
    where the festivals are impending with chariot races
and mock battles. The athletes are working out or soaking
    sore muscles . . . The theaters are all busy
with the new season's productions. The city's pulse quickens
    and its citizens feel their own quickening with it,
those happy souls who take its rich arrondissements
    for granted, as I did, myself, once.
Now, I look about me, watching the snow turn
    to mud, watching the ice melt beneath
a grudging sun. The grip of winter shows some sign
    of relaxing again. Ships will appear in the harbor,

and I shall go running down with the others to ask whence
     they've come, and what they carry, and whither bound,
and what is their home port. The answer is almost always
     a disappointment, the name of another savage
anchorage up or down this same barbarous coast.
     Only the rare captain has taken his craft
across the distant seas from the parts of the world where Greek
     or—even better—Latin sings in the air
with the ease of the wind's wordless wailing through the shrouds
     above the wordless menace of the crew
whom the angry gulls scold, fly off, and then wheel back
     to scold again. Sometimes a skipper or mate
with a civil tongue in his head can, for a glass of wine,
     retail the news or rumors he's picked up
from a fortunate wind beyond the straits of the Hellespont.
     I sit in the tavern with such fellows and hope
for word of some good fortune for Caesar that might occasion
     a triumph, rejoicing, or even some general pardon.
Have the Germans yielded at last, recognizing the power
     to which they must bow their stiff necks or die?
Has Tiberius taught them the lesson any fool should have learned
     from Julius Caesar? The man who brings me report
of such good news I shall drag at once to my table to serve
     the best feast Tomis can offer. My home
shall be his to command. Or say, my residence, rather,
     for Naso is not at home here. Scythia's only
a temporary abode—or else a burial plot,
     if the gods do not prompt Caesar to relent.

III, 13

Like a great stupid hound, loping across a field
    and leaping up to muddy me with his paws
while he slobbers over my face with a huge adoring tongue,
    my birthday god has found me and comes frisking,
even here in Tomis, misery's stronghold. The poor
    stupid brute! Had he the least sense
of shame or understanding, he'd have stayed in Rome,
    shown a little heart, and not followed me here.
All of my smart friends are gone, but this poor oaf
    never heard? Someone or other must
have hinted how kind it would be simply to say farewell . . .
    And I agree! His hounding me here is sad.
Did Caesar's anger extend to him? Is a spirit subject
    to an emperor's order of exile? All this way,
and it expects to be greeted, wants its accustomed honor,
    the white robe, the incense burning, the flowers
decorating an altar, and even the little cakes
    to signify the sweetness of the occasion.
It wants to be made welcome, to see me act like a child
    as people do on birthdays. The poor fool
must learn what life is like in Tomis. Altars here
    are better decked with funeral cypress. Words
of good omen would wilt and die upon my lips.
    Still, it has traveled far. I ought to respond.
For custom's sake and the day, I'll make one birthday wish—
    that it not find me here a year from now.
All natal and mortal creatures, doing time,
    have that gift of eventual release.

III, 14

Friend of the arts and artists, scholar, generous patron
    of whose kind notice I used to be proud,
only now do I learn the value of your esteem,
    independent, abiding—the way a friendship
always ought to be but seldom actually is.
    My books are still on your shelves, and you still speak
my ghostly name to the new poets coming along.
    Not just my spirit, but even my corpus
you keep alive and well in the city to which I write
    to thank you and offer the praise that you deserve.
Mine is the fervent gratitude a father would feel
    toward one who had done his abandoned children a
                                        kindness,
for those poems of mine to which you still give house room
    are children or rather orphans left behind,
to fend for themselves in whatever way they can on their own
    or with help—for you're their guardian now.
Three of my offspring carry the trait and share the taint
    of my corruption, but keep the rest of the flock
with the kind care you have shown them over the years. Remember
    the thrice five books of the *Metamorphoses,*
snatched, as it were, from the conflagration of my disaster.
    I think with remorse of what I left undone,
how unrevised it has limped into the marketplace.
    And find if you can a place for this new arrival,
the hayseeds still in its hair as it comes shambling in
    from the end of the world. I pray you bear in mind
how and where it came into being and make excuses
    for all its defects. To take up a pen here
is an act of defiance, folly, stubborn pride, habit,
    and the occasion of deep chagrin. There are no books,
nothing to prompt me here or prime the pump to flowing.
    There's no literate talk but only the rattle

of men in armor. Poets don't need enormous throngs
    but a small group to read to, intelligent ears
to appreciate and judge, sometimes to make suggestions . . .
    Not here. And neither is solitude,
that elegant private calm in which one might set to work
    and do one's best. I weep to admit how badly
I grope and fumble. I try for a word and can't think.
    I feel my Latin fading like an inscription
on a stone the wind is wiping back to its first blankness,
    and the wind is full of the grit of Thracian chatter,
Scythian jabber and terrible Getic gobbledygook.
    By a guttering lamp I go over these pitiful pages
looking for any solecisms or Pontine lapses.
    The guards at the gates are supposed to fend off the raids
of the Getic brutes on our outpost. I'm on guard as well,
    alert to their subtle incursions, but weary, weary . . .
It's not just a conceit: out here I am Rome.
    Think of me kindly, fairly, as you have
for many years, and consider my fate as you read over
    Ovid's lastest work, these halting plaints.

Book IV

For whatever gaffes and lapses you find, reading these verses—
    and they won't be hard to catch, strewn as they are,
thickly—I beg your pardon. Remember, I'm in exile,
    writing not for fame but solace, to work
my woe into an artifact, that change in its nature
    a kind of distraction better even than comfort.
So does the shackled slave, digging his ditch, sing
    as he swings his pick: the task remains the same,
but he is free and becomes his song, as the bargee does
    performing a mule's work on the cindered towpath,
tugging and singing. And galley oarsmen contrive to float
    on the purl of the very flute that sets their rhythm.
The shepherd perched on his rock passes the boring hours
    with his pipes of Pan. The household slave-girl spins
singing along with her wheel. The art is anodyne,
    as Achilles discovered, playing upon his lyre
after Briseis was gone. And Orpheus sang his dirges
    to which the rocks and rivers rang in chorus
after he'd lost Eurydice to Hades a second time.
    The same mercy the Muse has shown to me,
penitent here in the Pontus. She has been my friend,
    undeterred by Sintians, undismayed
by raging seas, howling winds, or the leaden skies
    of this vast waste. She knows what brought me here,
how much or how little blame for what happened long ago
    is properly mine, and has come along to comfort
for the wrong she did me then. And having no other solace,
    I accept gladly enough whatever she offers.
It's a terrible thing to admit—humiliating, really—
    but the truth of it is I'm much like a lover
who clings for dear life to the source of his pain. These scrolls
    and pens and ink I set out every morning

are dangerous implements, tricky to handle as any dagger.
　　　But even the mutilated soldier admits
that some weapons are handsomely made, attractive to hold
　　　in the hand and feel their heft and delicate balance.
So, I take up the pen in an exercise that appears
　　　mad, I suppose, but offers a certain advantage:
it occupies my mind, keeping my griefs at bay.
　　　It also makes my surroundings disappear,
which here is a blessing beyond all possible measure.
　　　I may yet turn into one of those curious creatures,
those priestesses of Bacchus who get caught up in their dance,
　　　insensible, ecstatic, and do not feel
the wounds they inflict on one another, shrieking in joy
　　　rather than pain, from which their ivy garlands
seem to protect them—and I sport that ivy too,
　　　the emblematic uniform of poets.
All the other gods have sided with great Caesar;
　　　only the Muse has cast her lot with me,
sharing my dangerous journey and present array of troubles
　　　as numerous as the sands of the seashore,
or the fish in the sea, or eggs in the roe in the fishes' bellies.
　　　To her I pray to give me the strength to continue
devising such figures. I notice springtime flowers
　　　if there is work in hand, and pay attention
to fields with their ripening crops, the yield of harvests, a first
　　　snow of the winter. They seem to glow with meaning
if, in my head, I have lit a lamp of artistic intention.
　　　Snuff that guttering flame and each sensation
is only an ache, each one very like the preceding
　　　but deeper and duller as I grow ever duller,
a hulk who is less and less deserving of human compassion.
　　　After a point, suffering turns absurd
and even provokes laughter from those who can no more bear
　　　its serious contemplation—I laugh too

to think of myself out here, living among the Bessi
    and Getae, I, an ornament of Roman
civilization. It is, indeed, a risible matter
    for me, who was never a fighter, to go about
with sword, shield and a helmet from which my gray hair shows.
    The fragile joke dies when the lookout sounds
a real alarm and I hear it and fumble my armor on
    with trembling hands and run, puffing hard,
to try to defend this accursed place from the savage raiders—
    or to stay alive, for if it goes we go.
There's nothing at all amusing about those enemy raids.
    They gallop back and forth along the walls
inside of which we crouch for cover and cower, watching
    for arrows dipped in poison—even a scratch
can kill a man. We're scared but know how lucky we are:
    outside the walls it's worse. A stray sheep
would have a better chance with a pack of wolves. One's throat
    is cut or one is shackled so he can be
led away as a captive. Here, at the world's bottom,
    we all have this uncomic fear of falling.
And even here in this extemity, the Muse
    pops up, a good old girl, my passion once
and more than a pal now, to see whether I still
    am worth her attention (or she can arouse mine).
So, yes, I still write, but feel like a fool.
    There's nobody here to read to, no one who knows
good from bad or even Latin from barnyard noises.
    I write for myself and read aloud to myself,
and approve—and feel terrible, whether I'm right or wrong,
    for it's awful either way, and the tears flow
and the lines writhe as the ink of the words on the pages runs.
    It's a game only a fool would keep on playing.
I ask myself over and over again why
    I bother, making an ass of myself this way

and, disgusted, I throw my work into the hearth to watch it
	burn as my soul burns, shrivel and turn
to ashes. These few poems you now hold in your hand
	are survivors, a small band who made it back.
Show them the kindness you would to wounded legionnaires
	limping from a rout back home to Rome.

IV, 2

Let us suppose a triumph—there's no reason not to.
	At this very moment, the Palatine
could be decked with garlands of flowers; incense might be burning
	in crackling fires to signal our great success,
the end of the German wars and submission at last of the wild
	hordes up there who always were an annoyance
until Tiberius managed to bring them under our yoke.
	There's no reason why I shouldn't assume
animals' throats stretched back for the sacrificial knife
	and the blood spattering forth, as great Augustus
and all his house offer friendly gods the thanks
	we all must feel. I can imagine it clearly,
the impressive tableau: beside Tiberius and Augustus,
	Germanicus and Drusus with their wives,
Livilla and Agrippina, and next to them, Livia,
	leading the women who chant thanksgiving prayers
before the Vestals' flame. Outside, the loyal plebs
	cheer and the knights look on from their enclosure . . .
That's where I would be if I weren't here at this table,
	making it all up but more and more
convinced that the vivid fancy is not merely mine
	but that of the Fates' too, a passing whim

that really comes to pass just as I say it is.
    I can almost hear the names of the captured towns
and their leaders' names and titles as they are read out to the crowd.
    I can see the chiefs march by in the slow procession,
with chains around their necks and chains of flowers
    around their horses' necks. Some of their faces
are grim; others are dazed and dull; still others betray
    the fear of what will happen next. Or their eyes
burn with the last embers of hatred's banked fires,
    and we recognize a worthy foe and ask
which one is that—commander, officer, priest, or spy?
    Between the displays of prisoners, come the floats,
representations of lakes, mountains, rivers, and forts,
    the names of which are familiar to us already.
There, that one, the woman with tresses flowing
    from her lowered head, is Germany, itself.
And there in the victory car Caesar is riding, proud
    in customary purple; the people cheer,
strewing his path with flowers, waving, shouting Hurrahs
    at the tops of their voices, and making his horses rear
impressively; and the people cheer again louder
    all along the route to the citadel
and Jupiter's shrine. From a thousand miles away, I see it
    as if I were there! And they can see me, too,
or at least I can let them imagine me imagining them,
    let them realize Ovid wishes them well,
rejoices as any Roman ought to do for a Roman
    victory. They can see into my heart
as surely as I can see into theirs, and have to know
    how glad I am. My timing, perhaps, is off.
It may not be at this particular instant—but who
    would blame me for anticipating a little?
What if it isn't now as I write, but the poem's now
    as it's being read in Rome? That wouldn't be bad.

My exile's vision is visionary; the mind's eye,
    wandering as free in time as in space,
can peer into either distance. I look to see Rome,
    but if I focus wrong may prophesy—
but only with good tidings (for which I take no credit,
    but for which I shouldn't expect censure). The crowd
is happy and I'm happy as we all maneuver and jostle
    for a better vantage. The ivory car comes,
and I want to see it, rub my eyes, and see it still,
    clear as before. I hear its wheels rumble,
loud as the knock at the door I know I am going to hear—
    the air is already charged with its echo—announcing
news from home, confirming every last detail
    of what I have written here. And I shall rejoice,
not for what it could mean in improving my situation,
    nor even in pride for my accurate predictions,
but simply as any citizen would, on such an occasion
    happy to lay his private griefs aside.

IV, 3

It is one of those clear nights when the stars appear to shine
    just out of reach. There is, of course, no moon,
and that's fine: the fickle moon is always changing,
    while the stars remain the same, and the two bears,
wheeling about forever but never deigning to touch
    even their paws in the restless sea, are constants
sailors trust with their lives. To them I make my appeal,
    for in their ample orbit the wide world
is embraced at once. They shine on me, here in Tomis
    and also upon those walls that Remus vaulted

before his brother killed him. They can look down on Rome
    on a night like this to beam into my window . . .
Is my wife there? Is she looking out, thinking of me?
    What, if the stars could speak, would they report?
Would I really want to know? Or dare? I swear I would.
    One must have faith in unwavering faith. Polaris
would be less likely to wander than she. I don't need
    the testimony of stars to what I already
know in the depths of my heart to be certain and true. She
    thinks of me and says her name aloud,
which is my name too, and gazes at my portrait
    to speak to me of her love. Providing only
that she is alive tonight, her love is alive.
    And if those stars could speak to her, they'd say,
when her heart is heavy, having braved its griefs all day,
    and woe sneaks up at night when she lays her head
on the pillow we used to share, that I love her still
    and wish I could reach out my hand to comfort
her tossing body. Our love expresses itself in aches
    instead of pleasures; morning's weary bones
are a parody of past mornings when, after passion,
    we'd drag ourselves from bed. The torture is all
we have left these days. It's what Andromache felt,
    watching Hector's body hauled in the dust.
I can't imagine what to pray for or what to want.
    Should I want you sad? Could I bear to be the cause
of your unhappiness? Do I want you not to be sad?
    But what kind of wife would you be then?
I wish a bearable grief for my misfortunes rather
    than yours. Weep for my woes. There's pleasure in it,
sweet release and relief. If you had been mourning my death
    you would have known that comfort, and my spirit
could have sailed forth, free, into the open air,
    while your tears wet my lifeless breast. The sky

on which my eyes had closed, gazing and then glazing,
 would have held your face like a constellation.
My ashes could then have been laid to rest in the family tomb,
 in native ground. This life I lead is worse
than any such death, for you are an exile's wife,
 and you look away and blush to be so called,
as I blush now. It is a misery, your shame.
 A misery, for you to regret our marriage!
Where is the time you boasted that you were married to me?
 Where is the time when you were proud to be seen
beside me in public? You don't hate to have such moments
 recalled, do you? I think of little else . . .
How happy we were then! And how you graced my life!
 You must never let your grief curdle to shame,
for which you have no cause. I could rehearse the stories
 of gods and heroes—Euadne and Capaneus,
or Semele and Cadmus. The fall of a husband or father
 is not contagious, carries no dreadful taint.
Indeed, the reverse is true—that there is a kind of challenge
 catastrophe brings. The old stories are clear:
glory is never the fruit of a happy and tranquil life.
 Without the Greek invasion, Troy would have been
better off, no doubt, but who would have heard of Hector?
 Without the raging storms to batter the Argo,
how could the strength and skill of Tiphys have been made
            known?
 Apollo's arts of healing would never merit
our admiration if men and women were always healthy.
 It's up to you, my dear, how you respond
to this dire occasion. I'm sure your greatness of spirit
 will shine as a beacon, guiding the lives of others
for years to come. That you speak out in my behalf
 does you credit, whatever people may think
of me and my sad case. Adversity is the only
 test by which virtue can prove itself

in action. Nothing else we say or sincerely intend
    is worth a damn. My exile here is your
fame, now and forever, a pedestal for your lofty
    monument, and a field of honor for love.
These waste expanses before me will bud and I'll watch them
                                                        bloom
    in bouquets of your richly deserved praise.

IV, 4

Sir, I refrain from inscribing your noble name here,
    but I don't at all—and cannot—by that omission
diminish in any degree the nobility of soul
    that corresponds to that of your name. I sing
praises clearly your own. To them you are entitled
    in such a way that I could never conceal,
no matter how I contrived to generalize, that you
    were the man I meant. Your qualities point you out
almost as well as your name: your eloquence speaks of you
    eloquently; your generous spirit gives
the testimony I might rather, for safety's sake,
    suppress. And yet I wonder whether the danger
is really so great. My homage is unlikely to cause
    embarrassment. Caesar is fair about such things,
has tolerated allusions I've often made to himself . . .
    He can't really prevent them, for he is the state
and the common good to which I still can claim rights.
    I mention Caesar in much the way I mention
Jupiter, subject of poets. And both of them are constrained
    to permit such liberties. So your risk

is small, given those august—not to say divine—
     examples. Still, assume a certain displeasure
on Caesar's part. He knows that you have no control
     over what I write out here. I'd be the one
he'd blame, if there were blame. For me to address you thus
     is nothing new. When I was still in Rome,
we often spoke. My infection did not touch you then;
     I doubt it will bother you now. At the very worst,
you can say what is anyway true and common knowledge:
     that you didn't seek me out but rather found me
among the family heirlooms, for I was your father's friend.
     He was my benefactor, approving my work
with that marvelous orotundity he was famous for.
     If any blame attaches to our connection,
let it be his whose safety—alas—is all too secure
     in the house of the dead. But I know you won't deny
our old friendship. You nature is too decent for that,
     and you understand my relegation here
was not for any crime, that my error may have been grievous
     but never my heart. I'm sorry! I've done that number
often enough before, and neither of us requires
     any further reminder of those details.
It's enough for me to say that I recognize the justice
     of my present condition, even as I deny
I ever intended anyone harm, as Caesar knew.
     He recognized this and therefore spared my life;
he never seized or gave away my family's goods,
     as he otherwise might have done. I cling to the thought
that I read his gesture correctly, that there is yet a hope
     his wrath may soften further and he may hear
my oft repeated plea that I be allowed to return
     part of the way—to a milder place of exile.
Having once spared my life he may not begrudge me
     comfort and safety too. There are lots of places . . .

Close your eyes and let your finger fall on a map
    anywhere. I'll go tomorrow morning!
Suggest this to Caesar. Make it a game, a joke,
    a moment's diversion. It would be my life,
a trifle and yet the greatest favor I can imagine.
    Sir, in the name of our friendship and for the sake
of my friendship with your father, speak the words, ask;
    find an appropriate moment, smile, and ask.
It will cost you nothing and bother the emperor hardly at all
    but it's everything to me. This terrible place
on the bleak shores of the Black Sea is a torment, torture.
    Black in aspect and omen, with its black-hearted
savage tribes . . . I can't expect you to believe
    the grim truth, but it's terrible here, hellish,
with cutting winds that never bring any better weather.
    The desperadoes who live here have no idea
of civilization, but love cruelty, violence, gore—
    which is all they see around them in angry nature.
The cult of Diana here makes human sacrifices:
    with game dear and human life worthless,
it makes a kind of sense. It was here that Iphigenia
    was carried from Agamemnon's altar at Aulis
to become priestess rather than offering in that same
    dreadful rite. It was here that Orestes came,
driven by furies, hoping to find someplace to hide
    where blood-guilt isn't even worth remarking.
It wasn't his crime but only his having come from abroad
    that marked him out as a victim. Thoas, the king,
sent him off to be killed with Pylades, his companion.
    And the priestess was Iphigenia! It's grotesque,
but the old myths carry a tang of musty truth
    all of us recognize. The story's correct
at least in its choice of locale. These long-odds narrow escapes
    suggest what the likelihood is: that the sister kills

her long-lost brother; and friend will vie with friend
    to try to survive. She stands there with the knife,
half drunk, ready to plunge the dagger down . . .
    and recognizes her brother! And then they flee
back to Greece with the statue they have to bring back to atone
    for everything that's happened. I think of this story
often, here in this bloody place. To be brought home
    by the same fair wind that brought Orestes
back to Argos, the god having been appeased at last!
    Such is my prayer. It could happen again.

IV, 5

Oldest and best friend, to whom I once turned
    at my worst hour, you gave me comfort then.
The flames of my hope danced as the flames on Minerva's altar
    leap when the priest pours on the sacred oil.
You never thought of your own safety, turning to prudence
    a deaf ear, but made your house a harbor
for a stricken vessel, hearing only my cries of woe—
    as a friend ought to do for a friend. Had Caesar
stripped me bare, I know you would have clothed and fed me.
    I feel your name prickle my fingertips
but for safety's sake restrain my grateful impulse to honor
    a decent man. You recognize yourself
and feel perhaps the temptation to proclaim, "I am the one."
    On another day when the weather improves, as I hope
it will, I'll revise this homage and set down your name
    in the name of friendship. Fame is the poet's gift,
or it ought to be. Meanwhile, you have my unpoetic
    (indeed, all but mute) thanks and love.

You are in my thoughts always. I conceive of us as rowing
    against the wind and tide. We're hardly moving,
but patience and faith must triumph. Winds shift and tides
    sooner or later turn. Our vessel will scud
along the tips of the waves, fast, light, and amazing
    both of us. Meanwhile, I wish you well,
trusting that you will never need the help you have given.
        May you and your wife enjoy one another's goodness,
and you and your brother share the fame of Castor and Pollux
    for fraternal amity. So, may your young son
grow up to be like you, and everyone do him honor
    recognizing in him his remarkable father.
And last, for your wonderful daughter, upon whom I know you
                                                    dote,
        may the marriage torch burn bright, and in its glow
you shine as a fond father-in-law and, soon,
    still in your prime, a grandfather, proud, and happy.

IV, 6

Time tames the ox to the weight of the yoke; time
    breaks the spirited colt to the bridle; time
even settles the wildness of tawny Phoenician lions
    to behave in the circus as if they were housecats.
Those great gray behemoths from the Indian jungles learn
    in time to obey their masters, bearing a howdah
and servitude. The famous soother and healer, time,
    is the vintners' ally, making the grapes grow
until they swell with juices near to bursting. Time
    ripens the ears of the farmers' grain and renews

the soil's richness too. What can it not do?
    Flint, and even the hardest diamonds, time
can grind away, as it also can soften the hardest heart,
    assuage the deepest grudge, comfort the greatest
grief. The art of time is to lighten, fade, and heal . . .
    But I have been out here now a long time,
have seen the harvest come and come again, have watched
    the grapes pressed into the vats twice,
but feel my heart as sore as the day I stepped ashore,
    my wound as raw, and my woe as fresh as ever.
It is not, after all, the perfect healer: an old bullock
    sometimes shies from the yoke; a broken horse
tries to avoid the snaffle. And my present despair
    is worse, bitterer, riper now than then,
having grown like a crop of these vile hardscrabble fields
    or the sour fuits of these gnarled and stunted trees.
My grief is richer and keener, familiar now like an old
    enemy who knows my every weakness
and how to exploit it, how to find those tender places
    to poke and prod and make the hurt nerve thrill.
When I was first sent away, I had the strength to bear it,
    but strength saps and I am worn down, worn out,
have less and less hope, less patience, less
    sanity left. The fresh wrestler bounds
lightly into the ring; my arms are lead. The fresh
    gladiator just entering the arena
stands tall; my armor is dented and stained red
    with my heart's blood. I am weak, weak to exhaustion,
and sick, knowing the next bout must do me in.
    A storm at sea will toy with a new ship
but wreck a weaker and older vessel. My timbers creak
    at each wave, and I know what the next will bring
or the next after that. I'm pale, thin, and my body
    is falling apart, but my mind is the trouble, is worse,

for I don't care. The idea of health is as far away
    as Rome itself where my friends are, and my wife.
I look out at a wasteland full of Scythian crazies
    and Getae in their curious trousers: Death
in silly costumes and funny hats, teasing and jeering.
    I kill time. And hope it returns the favor.

IV, 7

Twice has the ice thawed and the iron grip of winter
    relented to let the ships approach our harbor.
It's spring again, a time of rising sap and hope . . .
    How sappy is it for me to hope? Your letters
that I keep expecting, some few jotted lines from an old
    friend, never appear. I break the seals
when mail comes and look for your signature down at the bottom,
    but my hopes are always dashed. Is it just luck?
Deliveries are uncertain. It's possible that you've written
    often, but always in vain, your letters dispatched
only on ships that are wrecked or taken by pirates and burnt.
    Is it foolish for me to believe in some such story?
For the sake of our long friendship, I really have made an effort
    to do so. I can believe that Medusa's hair
was a tangle of vipers, that Scylla from the waist down was a dog,
    that there are Chimaeras half lion and half
snake. I am thought to be adept in the study of myths.
    I have persuaded myself that Centaurs exist
and that when we die we'll see a three-headed dog at the gates
    of Hades. The Sphynx, the Minotaur, the Harpies
trouble me not at all. I have devoted my life
    to these tall tales' poetic truth.

And I try now to believe in you and your steadfast affection,
    your thoughts of me, and your letters that never arrive.
But I need a little help. It's been a long time, old pal.
    Even an Ovid's stories begin to wear thin.

IV, 8

A crow turns into a swan . . . and you are expecting another
    extravagant account of a mythical marvel,
or heroic exploit, virtue rewarded or vice corrected.
    I wish it were anything else but the commonplace
occurrence that never surprises except in the looking glass:
    the hair at my temples is turning white. The icy
peaks of the years toward which I have been slowly ascending
    are here at last, and I look about and blink,
stunned by the harsh glare. From now on it's steeper,
    and the going gets harder. This is the time
when I ought to devote my attention to that ever more demanding
    expedition. Leisure, comfort, domestic
pleasures, the family gods are what men of my age
    think about, and perhaps estate planning.
I never gave much thought to what I would do in these last
    years of my life. I assumed, as most of us do,
that I'd conform somehow to conventional expectations,
    or at least I had no reason to fear worse.
How could any sane person guess what the gods
    had decreed? To be driven away, over land and sea,
to this suburb of hell? Could I have imagined that?
    Old ships are tied up at wharves and left
to decompose in the harbor, as horses are put out
    to pasture when their racing days are past.

Old soldiers are pensioned off and sent home to enjoy
    the peaceful life they have dreamt of on campaign,
and gladiators, surviving long enough to retire,
    are given a wooden sword that cuts nothing
but air. Like all of them I want only to rest,
    look back on my career (or maybe not),
sit in my garden, drink, and talk with a few old friends.
    It seems simple enough, but out here a marvel,
amazing as any miraculous transformation of those
    stories I used to recount. For five decades
the fates were kind, cosseting me in my prime, but now
    they have turned on me, turned mean, and harry my
                                                weakness.
Was I such a lunatic as would risk, so late in life,
    everything? (Should a lunatic be punished
with such harshness?) Caesar knows the extent of my fault,
    has shown his gracious mercy, spared my life,
and left me, even here, in this blasted outpost, hope
    which I have learned to grasp as one grasps nettles,
firmly or not at all. Belief in the whim of the gods
    is the lesson written large on the Black Sea blackboard:
nothing is so secure that Jupiter's thunderbolt
    can't at any instant blast it, and nothing
deserves reward or punishment. My fault is a part
    of my ruin, but greater by far is my having offended
divine power. That's hard for rational men to accept,
    but look around—at nature, the fates of men,
and at me. You don't reason with gods; you have to abandon
    intellectual pride and learn to pray!

IV, 9

Up to now, I've kept the names out of these poems,
    but I may make an exception for yours. I'd rather
forget you and what you've done to me, let it all
    wash down Lethe's currents, along with your tears
of chagrin that I'm still waiting to hear come gushing forth.
    People do crazy things now and again,
and I'm willing to let it go. But if you still nurse your grudge,
    continue to spew out the old venom
and to be a pain in the ass, you'll see what kind of acid
    I'll dip my pen into instead of ink.
Banished, yes, and far away at the borders of nowhere,
    but I'm still a Roman citizen with rights
that live on the Capitoline Hill and are able to reach
    to grab your scrawny neck. The oak that Jove
blasts is not always killed; sometimes it puts out new
    growing shoots. The Muse is still my friend,
even if you don't pay her a great deal of attention,
    and has her subtle strengths and her own weapons.
From all the way out here, on the edge of the Scythian wastes,
    these lines have managed to pass through rough country
like heralds reading out my complaint to all the world.
    If you were ever up before noon to see
the sun rise in the east, or sober enough in the evening
    to watch it set in the west, you'd get the idea
how far words can travel—in time as well so that you
    could go down to posterity as the scum
you really are. I haven't done it yet, but might.
    The arena's still quiet, but listen: that sound
is the bull in its stall, snorting for blood and pawing the ground.
    However you want to play it is fine with me.
You get, I trust, the idea. I await further word—
    or say that the Muse and I wait, together.

IV, 10

Let me conclude this sheaf with what might better have been
 its introduction—or mine. I've been assuming
readers will know who I am. Probably some of you do,
 or think you do—that clever naughty fellow
I used to be, the one who wrote so much about love.
 Well, yes, I was. But time has changed all that
and will, no doubt, make further revisions. Who knows whether
 in fifty years or in five hundred fame,
which is always fragile, will have deserted me utterly? Poets
 never know (it's probably just as well,
a circumstance that gives hope to more than it may discourage).
 For future readers, then, let me step forward,
clear my throat, and announce that I am a native of Sulmo,
 a few days' journey eastward from Rome, a place
of icy rushing streams. I was born in the year
 the two consuls, Hirtius and Pansa, fell
in the Mutina battles with Marc Antony. Our rank
 of knight goes way back. We condescended
to some of the recent equestrians. I was the second son,
 a year to the day younger than my brother.
We always had two cakes on the birthday we shared, and were close
 in other ways as well. We studied together,
and then went up to Rome to seek our fortunes together.
 My brother was smarter than I and a better speaker.
I used to waste my time trying to write verses—
 our father called it a waste: he disapproved
of any pursuit where you couldn't earn a decent living
 and always used to say, "Homer died poor."
He was right of course, as I knew then and still think now.
 I tried to give it up, to stick to prose
on serious subjects. But frivolous minds like mine attract
 frivolous inspirations, some too good

not to fool with. I kept returning to my bad habits,
    secretive and ashamed. I couldn't help it.
We assumed the toga together—if I felt like an imposter,
    I owed it to my father and brother to try
and do my duty. But then my elder brother died,
    just like that at twenty years old, and I
kept on trying but scarcely believed any more in myself
    or in anything I was doing. I wasn't cut out
for any of those serious, sensible public careers.
    I gave it all up and returned to the Muse
whom I had been anyway meeting in surreptitious trysts.
    Even my father accepted that I was a poet.
I was lucky at least in the timing of the choice I'd made. Macer
    was old then but I knew him well and heard him
read often of birds and snakes and healing plants
    from that long didactic poem of his. Propertius
was a close friend. We enjoyed poetry, conversation,
    and a friendly glass with Bassus, who used to write
iambics, with Ponticus famous now for his epics, and Horace,
    whose odes we heard him read with the ink still
damp on the page. I saw Vergil once at a party,
    but didn't have the nerve to go up to speak
to the great man. I knew Tibullus, but he died
    young—there are poems of his that I admire
but can hardly bear to read, missing my friend. That reverence
    I once felt for my elders, younger poets
soon enough showed me. My work was well received
    and I was invited to dinner parties. My father
could hardly believe it—neither at first could I, but one learns
    to take Fortune's greatest gifts for granted,
thinking that this is life, is merely what one deserves . . .
    I fell in love often, and married early.
It wasn't a good marriage and didn't endure long.
    My second wife was wonderful but she

died. And the third, my present wife, is my consolation
    in these times of trial. If it is in my power
to make her known as a legend of loyalty, I shall only
    be acting as clerk to take the world's dictation.
Blameless, she has suffered at least as much as I,
    and complained less, and never to me. Her daughter
has made me a grandfather, bringing me that joy
    that men share with the gods of reaching out
in pride of consequence to make a future. My father
    never lived to see his son's disgrace.
Neither he nor my mother had to watch their darling
    driven away—although, if spirits survive
the pyre, they've heard the reports in the Stygian court and know
    my relegation was punishment for an error
but not a crime. I'm getting old; my hair is mottled
    grayer now than when Caesar sent me out here
to the Black Sea and Tomis. It wasn't just my fame
    as a poet I thought was affronted, but my age:
fifty, and as I thought, deserving consideration
    not to say respect. I may not speak
of what happened, or even complain of former friends
    whose betrayal brought me to ruin here. I've learned
to bear it in silence (for me that's hard). But I have discovered
    we're tougher than we think, and can put up
with almost whatever we have to—the long journey, the cold,
    the arduous life, the constant danger. I hear
the din of arms from the very table at which I am sitting,
    framing these elegiacs to keep sane.
For a long time, I thought my father had been correct,
    telling me to keep away from this nonsense—
and he couldn't even imagine the extent of the dangers (success
    is just as risky as failure and either way
one takes his chances, playing a very long-odds game).
    I was furious at myself and angry at art,

hated the Muse, hated the look of unjustified type.
   But what has caused my misery has helped me
recover from the misery. The cure is still with Caesar,
   but the strength to get through the day is in these pages
arising from them and then settling back in tough
   sinewy Latin. I wonder how other people
who don't write bear their lives. I've learned to be grateful
   to the Muse whose mercy is hard but no less real.
With her help, I am able to leave the damned Danube
   and hover over Helicon. Her I thank
for a measure of fame that few but the dead are ever given.
   I've lived in a great time for poetry, seen
a lot, and know how talent doesn't always succeed.
   Envy, spite, grudges, favors called in,
and all the political games you'd find in the grand arenas
   of public life get played in the arts too.
The dead are accorded honor because they're beyond envy,
   as I seem to be out here, away from the action.
As good as dead, I've been granted by Caesar's decree a measure
   of fame I couldn't have otherwise expected,
though I don't altogether trust the odd combination of pity
   and notoriety helping my work get read.
But it can't hurt, can it? To be in this way promoted
   among the immortals (the poets, not the gods)
is agreeable. Some days, I lay down my pen, stretch,
   and go outside to tramp along the beach,
lean into the cold salt wind, and feel the earth
   solid under my feet, and I laugh, thinking
how it may not get me all. The best could survive for years:
   this profitless pursuit my father, who gave me
life, disapproved of greets you now, reader, with thanks
   for your attention by which I remain alive.

Book V

V, 1

Here comes another to add to the quartet I've already
    sent, a new collection of outland kvetches.
I'm sorry, my old friend, that I don't seem to have much range.
    I wish I could strike other notes from time to time,
but this is my life, its condition: I am mournful; my songs
    are mournful too as I try to keep to the truth—
anything else sounds silly and feels like a waste of time.
    I know I used to do other, more cheerful things,
some of which I regret and none I can even conceive of
    trying to imitate here. Since my disaster,
I am like one of those swans that are mute except at the end
    when they break their silence to sing their own dirges
in exquisite weakening notes in a gathering gloom. I imagine
    myself as one of those wonderful birds and hear
that thick silence around me. It's what my own death will be
    unless I perform my funeral rites myself.
Consider yourself warned: it won't be fun and games,
    naughty *double entendres,* witty conceits,
or any of those things I used to do. For that
    go to Gallus who always was good at it, try
Propertius, graceful and suave, or take a look at Tibullus
    or one of those people with whom I used to be
counted—and I was delighted to be compared with them—
    but now my smug grin has turned rueful
as I think what happened. My Muse may have fooled around but I
    was the one sent to the ass-end of the earth,
an amatory amateur no more, but a whiner,
    public nuisance, pest. And maybe a warning—
for if it could happen to me, to whom can it not happen?
    But there's no point in adducing reasons, which don't
apply. It isn't as if I were exercising a choice.
    I do what I have to do, from inspiration,

or—put it another way—from necessity, jotting down
    a few samples of anguish I undergo
every day. My only escape is here at the desk
    where I can pretend to distance my suffering, shape it,
mold and control it, triumph over it, just for a while . . .
    In other words, I'm writing for my life.
I hear you protest, "Naso, give us a break, will you?
    Isn't there any limit to your complaining?"
It's what I ask myself, but turning the question around
    to inquire what the limit may be to my hurting.
Ask the fates, the gods. Or, better, ask Caesar.
    Get him to bring me back to my wife and Rome.
Then watch me perk up. I'll write you cheerful poems
    (but nothing wanton—I've said goodbye to that,
and meant it). I will compose celebrations of life,
    paeans of praise Augustus himself will approve,
if only it can be worked to get me moved to another,
    less impossible faubourg of civilization.
But as long as I'm in Tomis, I'm likely to write complaints.
    What's odd is not that the tone tends to be woeful
but that I'm able to write poems out here at all.
    "Come on, old sport," you say. "Suffer in silence!"
as if there were some rule that victims of torture should not
    groan aloud, or the wounded cry out on the field.
There's nothing wrong with tears. Even Phalaris let
    the victims he was roasting alive in that bull
groan and bellow. Priam wept before mighty Achilles.
    Niobe wept, and Procne, and Philoctetes wailed
in his clammy cave. Weeping is perfectly all right.
    It's holding in your grief that can cause trouble.
The sorrow bubbles inside, boiling and then exploding
    to destroy mind and body, heart and soul.
You have to give me a little leeway, gentle reader:
    for me it's life or death; you have the choice

of walking away. Nobody's forcing you to read this.
    Do you exclaim how awful this is, how sloppy?
I agree. I urge you to put it aside. Drop it,
    read something with polish and wit. I would!
I'll tell you the truth: I don't even revise these things
    but send them out as they are, like beggar's children,
feeling a twinge maybe, but knowing that they'll do better
    because of their imperfections and how they affront
decent people's standards. They ought to look like hayseeds
    just blown in from the country on some ill wind.
My reputation? You think I still care about that?
    I'm not a Roman poet! Think of me rather
as the brightest and best bard of the Sauromatian school—
    judged by that standard, I'm a genius.
Then why, you ask, do I send poetry back to Rome?
    To be there with you, whatever way I can.

V, 2

And now what? Another letter arrives from the Pontus!
    And you turn pale and your fingers tremble as you
fumble it open, worried that the news will be bad. Good
    news would only come from the palace in Rome.
The best you can hope for is nothing new at all, the same
    report that I'm not ill, and in no worse spirits
than I was last week, last month—that all the other letters
    are still good. Pick one at random to read.
Nothing is changed. I'm maybe tougher than I once was,
    hardier, hardened (perhaps I'm only numb).
Inside, though, the hurt is as bad as it ever was.

There are some wounds that even time can't heal.
Small troubles, the little knocks and buffets, yes,
　　but the deep gashes fester, ooze, and stink
worse and worse. It's not what we'd prefer to believe,
　　and some of us deny what we can't bear,
but there it is—the world is sometimes a hard place.
　　Philoctetes languished there with his snake-bite
for ten years, throbbing an eternity of torment
　　with every passing minute. And Telephus suffered
and would have kept on suffering, failing, and then dying
　　if mighty Achilles hadn't supplied that rust
of his spear for the cure. It isn't exactly a cheerful story,
　　and the odds against that kind of happy ending
are very great. But I think of it often and recite it
　　over and over again, because it's the only
hope there is. Caesar must be the cure of my ills
　　as Achilles was . . . I've said that before, my love,
but there it is. Nothing is new, nothing changes.
　　I'm turning into a bore (which, for a poet,
is another kind of death), a monotonous pest. Does Caesar
　　want that to happen to me? I can't think why.
What could the benefit be to the glory of Caesar or Rome
　　for Ovid to gibber away at the end of the world
about his troubles, as many as shells on the beach, or roses
　　in a great bower, or seeds of the ease-inducing poppy,
or beasts in the woods, or fish that swim in teeming seas,
　　or birds in the air, or the feathers on all those birds?
By so many troubles am I ground down. Is that what he wants?
　　Does he know? Is it all to divert some middle-level
clerk in an office who writes amusing reports to his chief?
　　Is there any point in rehearsing yet again
the hardships of the trip? The dirt out here? The flies?
　　Or maybe they'd like a modest suppliant's prayer:

OVID'S PRAYER

Here I am, a poor creature, the lowest and furthest
        of all the humble voices that presume
to address themselves to the ear of a great and distant god.
        But if mere men can call upon Jupiter, I
can surely dare to pray to Caesar, Lord of the World.
        O mighty Caesar, invincible Caesar, protector
of the fatherland, the symbol of empire, and as great
        as the world you rule, I add my thanks and praise
that you deign to live on the earth. Some day you will rise
        to take your place among the stars in heaven
and twinkle down among the other smaller stars
        and other heroes' souls. I pray you, spare me,
let your anger mollify now, while it still can.
        Better that I should not have to mix my joy
with grief at your passing. I'm still proud to be called a Roman,
        and happy that in your mercy you moderated
my sentence which isn't an exile but only a relegation.
        I beg you, lying prostrate here in the dirt,
temper further your judgment, show me even more mercy,
        and let me go to a place where people speak
a civilized language. Latin is unknown here and Greek
        a kind of patois that gets mixed in with Getic
grunts. There must be some other out-of-the-way place
        where I might go. You could have had me killed
and didn't. You can't have intended for me to die out here.
        Fling me off of Charybdis, or hurl me into
Aetna's crater if that's what you want. Those would be quick
        and final—and better than this. Yours is the power.
It isn't punishment I complain about, or the torture.
        I'll take it like a man, whatever it is.
But the danger that's added on! I could die tomorrow . . .
        which is better or worse than what you intended for me.

I want neither more nor less than I deserve. I pray
    let me suffer elsewhere and in safety.

V, 3

Unless I've got it wrong, the calendars out here
    being at best approximate, today
is the festival of Bacchus, the day poets praise
    the genial god with garlands, cups of wine,
and songs made in his honor. O god, it used to be
    a wonderful time! I can remember a few
oblations that seemed at the time acceptable—if one judges
    the only way I know, by how the party
went, and how much wine was drunk, and how late it lasted.
    Pious and reverent, indeed! And now I write
from under the hind end of the lesser bear as it hunches
    down in the sky. You remember me, Ovid,
your old and devoted friend? Can't you help me out?
    Is it true that the Fates' decrees are beyond the gods'
powers? Can you at least put in a good word somewhere?
    Forgive, I beg, the impiety, but we
have a lot in common. You suffered much and traveled far,
    to the ends of the earth even as far as the Ganges,
enduring many trials. You're said to have passed through
    this dreary spot—in which case you
would feel sympathetic. It's not as if we were strangers!
    I'm one of the old gang. Haven't you noticed,
among the voices that used to surround your altar, mine
    is missing? Help me, Bacchus, I pray in the name
of every wineskin I've ever emptied or goblet I've drained.
    In the name of the boistrous Satyrs in your train,

for one of whom at my best moments I might have passed,
    do me this kindness and hear in their shouts and laughter
my thanks. In the name of the frenzied Bacchae and all wildness,
    remember me. I, too, am one of your own.
You smite those who offend you. Lycurgus cut down your vines
    and you let him think his own foot was a vine
so he hacked at that, too, with his mischievous axe and died.
    You punished Pentheus, King of Thebes, who disturbed
the orgies of the Bacchae—who tore him in little bits,
    and as he died he recognized his own
mother shrieking for blood. I don't ask for vengeance,
    but mercy rather, the kindness of inns and taverns.
Speak to Caesar, a god to a god, and urge him to grant
    my plea to be moved to a better place. And the poets,
all of whom you can count among your followers, order
    to drink a health to Naso, their bowls of wine
watered by tears—for me and what has befallen me
    and could happen to them. Let those who ever approved
something I wrote, or those whose work I praised remember
    how it's supposed to be among us poets:
we ought to help one another, show some loyalty, kindness . . .
    When they are in their cups, Bacchus, prompt them
to quote a couple of lines of mine, then look around
    to ask, "Where's Naso?" and then remember
as freshly as if it had just happened yesterday evening
    the banishment. Some few will consider writing
petitions, perhaps. I don't rely on that or expect it.
    All I ask for now is to be remembered,
that my name be kept alive in the minds of my old friends.
    To those who think of me, show your favor, grant
inspiration, give them the happiest turns and tropes,
    and invoke Apollo's favor for their work.

V, 4

I can imagine how this letter is going to look
      months from now when it arrives at last
in Rome, limp, wrinkled, the grime of the journey on it.
      A miserable looking thing, and yet
lucky to be there at all. I am its father and author
      and feel the pang of envy. Will my friend
know how I sealed the wax? Lovers and friends kiss
      their signets before they make their marks, but I
wipe damp cheeks with my ring. The salt tang
      isn't the bracing Euxine air but tears.
My friend, of course, will assume that I'm dejected as ever—
      correctly, I'm afraid. He never asks
how I'm doing, but then only a fool would inquire
      of me on such a topic, one who would need
someone to point out the sun overhead in the sky.
      If a fellow can find a leaf in a forest, a blade
of green grass in a meadow, or something to drink in a lake
      he can probably figure out how I'm doing.
Did anyone ask at the end of the *Iliad*, "How is Priam?"
      Did anyone send postcards to Philoctetes,
"Hope you are happy and well and having a good time . . . "?
      I wish I were dumb enough so I couldn't imagine
what suffering could be, just couldn't understand it.
      It seems sometimes that I must have been like that,
but you never were. You were always sympathetic and decent,
      and as able to feel another man's pain as your own.
You never had to ask, but instantly could intuit
      how someone felt and knew the right thing to say—
and what not to say. I owe you a great deal,
      but most for your understanding. I'm trying hard
to learn to bear with patience those misfortunes the god
      has visited upon me. I don't despair

that he may yet have a change of heart, or allow his own
     inclination toward mercy to plead my case.
But as much as patience or hope, it's your friendship that keeps me
     sane and gives me the courage I need to stand it
and the will to live. As Achilles had a friend in Patroclus
     I have a friend in you, but being less
noble and less deserving, I am all the more grateful.
     I often think of the few who stuck by me
that terrible day . . . A few? Call it a generous couple.
     But you were there, your face as wet with tears
as mine was, and as much in need of comfort as I.
     Whatever happens, I will remember that
to my dying day and perhaps even beyond that.
     There isn't any petition or even a hint
here at the end. This letter will speak clearly enough,
     looking like a scrap of paper the wind
blew in from the gutter. It will move you more than verse.
     You'll know what to do and will do what you can.

V, 5

This is the brightest day of the year, the one occasion
     for putting thoughts of my misfortunes aside
and rummaging through the trunks to find those white robes
     of celebration. Today is my wife's birthday!
I'm happy for her, rejoice on her account, and wish
     for a golden tongue to trill like a blithe bird.
I can't have forgotten how. The words must still be there
     waiting to be discovered again, dusted,
polished, and put in order to make a pretty bauble.
     I'll sing of the outdoor altar, its hearth hung

with garlands of braided blossoms. Bring me the incense, boy,
  and fetch me the wine. Already, I can hear it
hiss as it hits the blaze that burns in her birthday shrine.
  A great day! I welcome it, even here,
as it dawns bright and clear, and yet without affront
  or mockery. I pray to the day's spirit
to treat with loving kindness her whose day this is,
  your daughter. Promise her good things in the year
to come, health and respect, and let her enjoy her home,
  her daughter, Perilla, her grandchildren, her country . . .
all those precious things I feel bereft of here.
  I can't unselfishly wish her husband home
but I hope the other parts of her life may be trouble-free.
  A hundred years! And let her know I love her
as much as in that first hour we met, long ago.
  The fate that keeps me away from her is mine
and I hope its taint continues to keep away from her too.
  Nothing is certain for man. Who would have guessed
I'd be performing these rites here in the land of the Getae?
  But see how the breeze carries the rising smoke
that spirals up from the altar. The incense drifts westward
  across the huge sky and home toward Rome.
Smart smoke! It knows what's good for it. The omen
  is favorable: it gets the hell out of here.
I used to dismiss that kind of thing as mere superstition—
  the story about the ashes of those two brothers,
of Polynices and of Eteocles, and how
  those ashes recoiled, reformed to make the two
separate piles. I think it's Callimachus who says this.
  I supposed he was being fanciful and absurd,
but extremity teaches us much, enlarges our poor notions
  of what can happen, extending our belief,
or restoring it rather to what it was when we were children—
  as we are, still, all of us, Fortune's children.

This is the happy day when I do not think of complaint,
    but of her, and of my good fortune being the husband
of such a splendid woman. This must have been the day
    Andromache was born, and Penelope.
Their spirits surely presided over my wife's appearance
    onto the world's stage. I shouldn't wonder
that this is Alcestis' birthday as well. Loyalty, virtue,
    and every strength of character, every grace
seems to be in the gift of the genius of this day.
    I only wish that joy were a part of it too,
but how would those other noble qualities show themselves
    except through trials of adversity? Ulysses,
happy and safe at home, might never have come to know
    what an amazing woman shared his bed.
If Protesilaus hadn't died on the sands of Troy,
    we'd never have heard of Laodamia's love,
who killed herself to be with him, even down in Hades.
    But don't do that. You don't deserve to suffer.
Indeed, it's for your sake that Caesar may pardon me,
    unwilling to let an innocent woman grieve.

V, 6

And you, old friend, good friend, do you abandon me now?
    Does the fixed star of my soul's sky wobble?
Am I to believe now in nothing and no one, trust
    nobody's love or friendship or honor? Do you
consign me to such a view of life—which I can't avoid
    without your continuing help? I know I'm a burden,
but there's nothing I can do to change my situation
    (the gods know I would if I could), and you,

having once taken me up, ought not discard me now.
    Better that you had never held out your hand
in welcome than now, when I need you, to thrust me away or
                                      drive me
    from the altar of your household's private gods.
Did Palinurus desert the ship? Did Achilles' driver
    beg to be excused? Are all those stories
nothing more than moral exempla for little boys?
    Am I going mad out here? Can I trust my own
judgment, my deepest feelings? I honestly don't understand . . .
    I beg you not only for my sake now but yours,
for the sake of your own character, think about it again!
    I've never hurt you, never betrayed our friendship.
All I've done is get myself sent away into exile,
    which has its effect, I'm sure, but I'm not nuts.
And even if I were, did Pylades ever abandon
    Orestes at his worst and craziest moments?
I don't compare myself . . . But yes, damn it, I do!
    We make way, don't we, for both extremes,
good fortune and ill, standing aside for the blind,
    just as we do for the great men in their togas
with the wide purple stripes and the lictors running ahead
    holding out the bound *fasces* and shouting
Animadvertite!—Make way! And, of course, we do.
    If I don't mean much to you, then my fate,
my suffering ought to command a certain degree of that same
    respect. Does nothing impress you? Is nothing sacred?
Or do you perhaps suppose that my agonies aren't great
    and burdensome? I assure you—as many as bees
stirred up and swarming out of their hive, or ants
    streaming into their holes with their grain. I'm not
exaggerating, I tell you. The sands on the shore are minutes,
    and they're all burning my bare soles like hot
needles. Doesn't it matter? Can you think of a former friend
    in such desperate case and feel nothing,

no sympathy, no sense of duty, nothing
    at all? If that can be, then I am lost,
the last man alive on a floating hulk, and waiting
    only for finicky death to take me too.

V, 7

From the place where the Danube flushes into the Black Sea,
    I send you greetings, glad you're alive and well.
My dearest friend, you have been a beacon lighting the murk
    my life has become. Don't even ask how I am.
Reporting my woes in detail won't make me feel any better,
    and you'll be a lot worse off. So let it drop,
as I have devoutly wished to be able to drop it myself
    into the bilious sea. Suffice it to say
it isn't a good idea to offend Augustus Caesar.
    The country here is grotesque, the people savage,
the weather awful, the customs crude, and the language a garble
    that more or less resembles intestinal sounds
of an ailing goat. Tomis was once a Greek city
    but the Greeks are not stupid and most of them left.
Then the Getae moved in, barely pacified, barely
    civilized. One sees them scamper about,
bareback, quivers and bows on their backs, their arrows dipped
    in venom, their faces covered over with hair,
and the hair on their heads so shaggy they look rather like human
    bushes. They all carry knives at their belts
and you never know whether they're going to greet you or stab
                                   you,
    cut out your liver, and eat it. Among such people
your old friend, Ovid, the dancing-master of love,

tries to keep from hysterical laughter and tears
the occasions for either of which are practically permanent here.
    I'm happy to have your news—that my old poems
are still being read and sometimes even being performed
    in some theatrical version with dance and mime
in crowded theaters with real people clapping their hands.
    I used to joke about how vulgar it was
for playwrights to have their audience right in the room with
                                               them,
    but I'm not complaining now. That anything sticks
in oblivion's craw is welcome news these days. My name
    is still on people's lips? My eyes blur
with grateful tears. Poetry brought me to this sorry
    extremity, and perhaps it will bring me home.
At least it will hold me together, a recognizable self.
    I write here, rather a lot—there's nothing
else to do; there are no temptations, no distractions.
    Another kind of person might look to nature
to occupy his time, the novel flora and fauna
    inviting scientific observation.
But it's a desert here, and there's nothing much to observe.
    Sociology? Anthropology? No,
neither of them is tempting, given these gross tribes
    that sweep down from the steppes to attach themselves
like body-lice on the hindquarters of civilization.
    They're dangerous, ugly, mute, and smell awful.
Their only law is that strong men can dominate weak.
    Their customs are less refined than those of wolves,
albeit in sheep's clothing in which they wrap themselves too.
    A few of them understand some words of Greek,
but mostly I've learned to speak Sarmatian—I get by
    with a combination of phrases, gestures, and nods.
My Latin, I fear, is getting rusty and stiff. I expect
    you'll find here and there infelicitous phrases,

awkwardnesses, barbarisms . . . They're not my fault
    but that of this outlandish place. I walk
on the beach sometimes to declaim the poems I know by heart
    to try to keep my tongue and the Latin tongue
conformable in my mouth. I talk to myself out loud,
    as madmen do in Rome, but here to stay
sane. Sometimes I stop at a word whose precise meaning
    escapes me for the moment, and I feel the fear,
the impotence and the rage that the very old feel
    when their minds start to go, and the tears come . . .
It's a hell of a life, my friend. But I hang in there, singing
    like a little birdie does—or maybe a crow.

V, 8

Lowest of low, lower than lowest, you are immense,
    a phenomenon, man! I'd thought I had fallen as far
as a person could fall, to the very bottom of life's barrel.
    But under the barrel, look, there is a slug,
and underneath the slug, there is slimy nasty stuff,
    and there you are, underneath that. Amazing!
To mock someone like me, despite the fact that I suffer,
    or rather because I suffer—what kind of beast
wouldn't display compassion to a poor fellow creature
    in such distress? A mad dog will relent
when the animal it has attacked offers its throat, but you
    have no such limits. Fortune may yet teach you
a little of what you need to learn. The giddy goddess
    on her dizzying wheel delights in such reversals,
as Nemesis loves to bring down those whose arrogant pride
    invites her severe attention. People who laugh

at shipwrecks often drown, and the rest of us have to approve
      the justice of it. Those who mock at beggars
wind up sucking stones and feeling their bellies
      growl and grumble, exacting a cruel revenge.
You think it can't happen? I was once riding high;
      I had my day, but that kind of roll can't last
any more than a fire one makes of straw—it burns
      bright but quick, and then it's colder than ever.
There still could be another shuffle and deal, and I
      might come back. Caesar could change his mind
at any moment, bring me home, grant me a favor,
      whatever I want . . . And I shall remember you,
and make you the proper gesture of recompense for your long
      and unremitting hatred. Poetic justice?
I am a poet, remember, and sometimes we make suggestions
      that those with the real power find engaging.
But better than that, I'd rather simply stand and watch
      as you bring yourself down, which is more than likely.
Given the kind of hemorrhoidal ass-hole you are
      in your nasty heart, I'd bet a bundle on it.
I may even send a note expressing my deep regret
      that I can't be with you at such a trying time.

V, 9

What can one say in a poem? What, for that matter, can one
      say in what we refer to as real life?
When I was back in Rome, I could have said to your face
      what I'm trying to write now—but that would have been
terrible form. And now, from a thousand miles away,
      it isn't a whit easier to declare

how much I am in your debt. Anyone reading my poems
     ought to see your name on the title page
along with mine. It was your kindness that made it happen.
     Without you, I couldn't have managed a line.
And now that my life has fallen into this sudden abyss,
     your loyalty rivals your kindness. A freezing man
understands what we consider unremarkable human warmth
     as a wonderful blessing, and he is of course correct.
Such greatness of spirit as you have continued to show me
     shouldn't go unrecognized. I only
wish I could inscribe your name in capital letters.
     My hand is like a hound that has caught the scent
of the deer's fresh trail, or like a horse in its stable
     skittish with want of exercise and nudging
the stall door with its head, and pawing the floor with its hoof.
     But I must restain my impulse, for your sake—
your own modest inclination, and my concern
     for your safety. Still, you know who you are, and know
there isn't a day that passes in which I don't feel affection
     and gratitude for what you have done and continue
still to do. It keeps my spirits up, and I owe you
     yet again, compounding my ruinous debt.
I write to wish you well. May the gods and Caesar keep you
     safe and happy and show you their friendship. A greater
prayer I cannot frame. It's the custom among these tribes,
     when a man saves another's life in battle,
that the one who has been saved presents himself as a slave.
     It's a real offer and sometimes is accepted.
It's one I'd make if I could, or rather it's one I do
     indeed make, knowing you can't refuse
from such a distance. There isn't much I can do for you—
     but what I can, I will, as long as I live.

V, 10

I've been here, it seems, forever. Three times already the Danube
    has hardened to dull metal; three times has the bilge
of the Black Sea turned solid. It feels like a lot more,
    like the ten years the Trojans were under siege.
Time is peculiar here, with a draggier pace. What runs
    with the grains of sand in an hourglass in Rome
oozes here like tar. The summer solstice does not
    shorten the days, or the winter shorten the nights.
The seasons here come late, as if they too were reluctant.
    Not that I blame them. Nothing would volunteer
for duty in these parts. Trees are extremely rare—
    apparently they have sense and are unwilling
to put down roots in such a place. The sinister bank
    of the Black Sea? It's aptly enough named.
The wild tribes that charge down from the north think it
    unmanly to support themselves by working,
preferring to raid and plunder. They assume we're here
    like the game in the fields, and they have only to take
whatever they like. Our farmers must wear swords to plow.
    The shepherds go out in armor and listen for hoofbeats
as much as for howling wolves. We live from day to day,
    from moment to moment, always a little afraid.
Whenever we get complacent, the savages seem to know it
    and swoop down like a flock of birds of prey—
and when they do it's every man for himself out here.
    Sure, we have some soldiers and all belong
to a kind of ragtag militia, but mixed among our numbers
    are a great many Getae who've settled here, willing
to swap some of their wildness for what they consider comfort.
    Loyalty isn't part of the deal. They don't
know what it means—or even have a word in their language
    to signify such a thing. They are brutes, beasts,

wearing the hides of beasts, are shaggy and smelly and crude . . .
    Those few who are able to claim descent from the Greek
colonists who founded this place so long ago
    dress in trousers like Persians, and speak less Greek
than I speak Sarmatian or Getic. And Latin words
    produce blank stares. They think me outlandish.
I have to use gestures and nods, point, and play charades
    with these stupid semihumans who laugh at me.
I know they do, and I'm sure they are often talking about me,
    making fun, not even behind my back.
I smile a lot as if I understood what they meant
    and took it as a joke, but inside, seethe.
I hate them all. I despise them! But I still have to be careful.
    Everyone here is armed to the teeth, and fights
break out in the public streets two or three times a day,
    with people maimed or killed. Sometimes I wonder
how I've survived this long. It must be Lachesis' joke
    to spin out my life's thread and with it my exile
to exquisite length, as if my suffering were amusing.
    Every moment's a blow, an affront, torment.

V, 11

My heart breaks, or rather I feel my stomach sinking
    and it's hard to catch my breath as I read your letter.
That someone insults you like that and calls you "an exile's wife"
    is mean of course, but also inaccurate—wrong.
It pains me, though, to imagine how you must have been hurt.
    My own woes I have learned more or less to bear,
but that I am the cause of your shame is awful. I hate it.
    It makes me ill to think of it. Bear up,

I beg you, my dear, for my sake as well as for yours.
　　　It isn't true, as you know. I'm not an *exile.*
My ship is disabled but not sunk. I'm still a Roman.
　　　My rights weren't taken away or my property seized.
I may have deserved worse, but Caesar was feeling kindly
　　　and showed me mercy. Look around you! The house
is proof against such malicious assaults as the one you report.
　　　It's still ours, yours and mine together.
Remember that terrible day? Who could ever forget it?
　　　Relegated, he said, which was bad enough.
But that was all there was. You aren't an exile's wife,
　　　and anyone low enough to say such a thing
ought to be beneath your notice. I know it hurts.
　　　I'm hurting, myself. But stick to the truth,
and use it has a shield: It's certainly hard enough.
　　　I'm alive, well, and writing in praise of Caesar,
whose mercy after all we have both received. I pray
　　　he may continue to show you no less kindness.
To the other gods I pray that they may give you a long
　　　life and freedom from such hurt. And for him,
the author of that slur, I want what he deserves—
　　　that his last lying breath is already drawn.

V, 12

You think I ought to devote my time out here to writing,
　　　to get through the bitter season and keep my talent
honed to its fine edge? I expect you mean well,
　　　but that advice you give me, my friend, is hard.
Poems ought to be written in a better frame of mind,
　　　joyful, content, or at least reflective and tranquil,

but not in actual pain. You're asking Priam to frolic
        at Hector's death or Niobe to dance.
The only appropriate art out here is that of the dirge.
        Poetry oughtn't be used as a hiding place
or lunatic asylum. That would demean the Muse
        and I should feel terrible having imposed.
It isn't right to abuse a hostess's invitation
        and turn her social evening into a market
for political favors or business deals. I feel the same
        punctilio for the art that has been so kind
so often in the past. Besides, my talent is stiff,
        injured by long disuse, like a fallow field
that hasn't felt the blade of a plow or been fertilized
        for years. Or I am a horse that's been kept too long
in his narrow stall. My case is probably even worse,
        for my mind isn't reliable any more.
I don't trust my emotions. Depression often does that.
        I take up the paper sometimes . . . I do. I try.
But nothing comes, or the lines are awkward and deformed,
        appropriate for their author's condition, but hardly
fit to be shown to the world. I throw them into the fire,
        more often than not. It doesn't make much difference.
I don't care about fame any more, or even praise.
        I'd just as soon that no one had ever heard
of Ovidius Naso. Obscure, but living in Rome, I'd be
        enormously better off. What has the art
ever done for me but get me sent out here?
        Groans are my art now, and bellows and whines—
as if the noises Perillus made from inside the bull
        when they lit the fire underneath it were art.
Even so, I'm tempted every so often. I think
        I might try it, but then I have to decide
in what language? I hear not a word of Latin in Tomis.
        The Greek is what you'd expect on a vaudeville stage

from somebody trying to get easy laughs as a bumpkin
  with straw in his hair. Sarmatian is not inviting,
or Getic, which sounds like the noises mating donkeys make.
  So I take a walk. Or go for a drink or two,
or even more than two. The impulse usually passes.
  But not always. Sometimes I have no choice,
and against my better judgment, I do take up the pen,
  knowing what violence I'm likely to do to the Muse,
my reputation, my own standards of taste and decorum.
  I'm driven to it, knowing I'm going to whimper,
screw up the metrics, commit blunders of diction, provoke
  pity and scorn, which are hardly what one wants.
I tell myself that I'm not committed to publication,
  that I can always throw away what I don't
really think is okay. And most of the time I burn them
  and have even learned to take some satisfaction
as I watch the words writhe and then ascend like prayers,
  which is hardly inappropriate. Still there are times
when I read what I've just written and have to admit to myself
  that I've caught a piece of the truth, awkward perhaps,
even ugly but still, for all its deficiencies, honest
  and maybe worth keeping—or else I lack
the moral courage to do what I ought and throw it away.
  But I can't. I'd sooner throw myself away,
and, believe me, I've considered that possibility too.
  And what I tell myself at such dark moments
is that it doesn't make any difference. Why not keep it?
  Why not let it stand? Sometimes, I do.

V, 13

From far away, I raise my glass to send you a *Health,*
    if one can send what he doesn't himself have.
My own decrepitude is all pervasive; it starts
    deep in my soul and spreads outward from there
to my body's furthest reaches. My side aches, my back
    is sore, my feet hurt and my nose drips.
It's the cold I guess, but that doesn't ever bother my neighbors.
    If you are well, I'm heartened, which could improve
my mood and my health too. You've only to let me hear
    that life goes well for you back in Rome, and I'm sure
my week would be made, my month. I'd feel like a new man.
    The proofs of your kindness have been so frequent, I wonder,
whenever a long time goes by and I haven't received
    a letter or even a note—are you okay?
I don't accuse. I'm sure you've written and put in the mail
    a number of letters that all have been lost. It happens
often enough. It's more likely than that your heart
    has hardened or you've forgotten your old friend.
I can't imagine that. It simply can't be true.
    Absurd! It's unacceptable. I reject it.
Still, I write to let you know how it starts to seem,
    that the thought, unbidden, arises for me to fight with
and argue away. It's not the pleasantest thing in the world,
    and hardly like old times when you and I
would talk about life and art on those rainy afternoons
    until the lamps were lit, and keep on talking
as they guttered lower and lower. In just that way, our letters
    ought to continue our conversations, the words
crawling on paper now that used to fly through the air.
    It's not what I'd have chosen, but still is better
than nothing at all, which is what I am now beginning to fear.
    Is that what's going to happen? I can't believe it!

I send you again a *Health*. May your fate be better than this
  of your old friend who trusts that you fare well.

V, 14

I have been looking these pages over, my dearest wife,
    and I see what a monument I've erected here
to honor you. What small satisfaction I'm able to take
    from this dejected, depressing work of mine,
comes from the truth of my representation of your virtues.
    As long as people anywhere read Ovid,
you can be sure of the fame your character has deserved.
    If I am a sorry figure, you're still splendid,
a light for time to come, and a model for all women
    to remember and emulate in moments of trial.
Other men can offer their wives expensive gifts,
    but nothing those women wouldn't be glad
to trade for a chance at the immortality you'll have.
    I'm happy for that. To have carved you a place in the annals
of civilization is no small thing and the least I could do
    after what you've done for me, the sole
guardian of my fortunes and vessel of all my hopes.
    My sorry condition is proof of what you've lived with,
showing devotion, courage, forbearance, and even love,
    all the way. My disgrace is the base,
the pedestal for your figurine on the temples' altars.
    Courage without danger to show it off,
or loyalty lacking trials or tests . . . They're easy enough,
    but your demonstrations, which I've been obliged to watch
and admire even though they broke my heart, are amazing.

It may turn out that I'm your story's footnote
which is perfectly fine with me. As long as Latin is spoken,
    and as far as the highways of Rome extend, from here
to the furthermost parts of Gaul, your name will be invoked
    along with those of Penelope and Alcestis,
for selflessness and the faithful love that cynics doubt,
    but I can swear exists because I've seen it.
I write to let you know how my adoration grows
    as if you were a demigoddess, but still
my human love remains undiminished from what
    it was on the day we parted. I'd add my thanks,
but that would be wrong. You'd only wrinkle your brow, puzzled,
    entirely unaware of having behaved
in any remarkable way. You haven't acted well,
    or even at all. Your nature expressed itself
in its pure spontaneity as a bird in miraculous grace,
    wheels overhead and astonishes us all.
I stand here on the shore of this bleak coast, observing
    a gull turn on the air, and I think of you.
My eyes brim. My heart brims over. I send my love
    and praise that I hope will last a thousand years.

EPISTULAE
EX PONTO

FOR ELENA

*. . . with subject, verb, and object dancing now
behind her glittering eyes.*

Book I

I, 1   To Brutus

Naso, again—by now an old hand here, who takes
     pen up once more, still penned up in Tomis
to send from the unmetaphorical Getic littoral these
     letters. Poems. Fugitive pieces. Hide them!
Stick them behind some boring book on an upper shelf,
     but keep the poor dears who cannot hope
for a welcome in libraries. Those public doors are barred
     by the name their cover carries, anathema now.
In a private house, you may make your own more liberal rule,
     and perhaps find them room in the vacant space
my *Art* once filled—that is now a dark ominous slit.
     I imagine your troubled look as you wonder what
I'm up to now. Relax! I promise, it isn't love;
     no more of that. It's my latter tristiferous note,
although not on the title page: I want not to be redundant,
     and the Black Sea is somber enough to suggest
a mood other than blithe. The important change in name
     comes at the top line of each of these pieces
where your names, like it or not, now appear *en clair.*
     These aren't parlor games I'm devising here,
and to hear that it's now a diversion to try to figure out
     to whom my complaints are addressed . . . It is obscene!
Far worse than any impropriety I
     was ever accused of committing! What obtains?
I'd thought to protect my friends, but the law permits these poems
     to circulate as freely as, say, the writings
of an Antony or a Brutus, whose far larger names
     (and blacker too) than mine don't seem to stain
the fingers that turn their pages. And Caesar himself cannot
     object to the message I send, for I have become
a holy man, a crazy who rattles away with a prayer wheel
     in front of the god's temple. Who can deny

one of those poor creatures a copper? You and I
    have passed them in the streets, have managed not
to recoil at their whines and groans, and have pitied their
                                 desperation—
    for how long were the chances that some god
to whom they offered up their repentance might relent,
    restore their sight, cure their lameness, soothe
their sores? We turned the corner and put it out of our minds
    that some of the gods seem to have a taste
for the keenings of their victims that attest their divine powers.
    I have been burned by the sun, been frozen, tempered,
refined and changed out here, in this land of inhuman extremes.
    My groans have taken on a public dimension,
as my career has become a cautionary tale.
    It isn't merely the torment of the exile
but the greater torment of knowing that I brought it on myself,
    that I have deserved what has happened. The sentence may
one day be commuted, but never the burden I bear
    of fault. Neither the clemency I pray for,
nor yet the death I fear, can ever expunge that taint.
    Are you perhaps surprised to hear me report
how my heart has softened, my attitude changed, my pride
    gone? Even the snows of this wasteland
melt at last and its rivulets gleam in the wan sun.
    Similarly, my heart melts. Or is gnawed
the way the ships in the harbor can have their ribs gnawed hollow
    by that mollusk whose name I can't remember that bores
from within so that seaworthy timbers no longer hold,
    and the ship founders. Or, better, think of the sea
itself and how its waves can hollow caves in the cliffs,
    battering rock away. Or look how rust
will eat iron to lace. Or worms masticate pages
    of books, reducing poetry to dust.
And so, with me, with my human heart that is not wood,
    stone, iron, or even parchment, but mere

meat on which sorrows raven until they have sated themselves.
    And when will that day be? Never! For I
have joined with the guards, have become my own chief
                                 tormentor,
    the shrewdest, the severest of them all.

I, 2   TO MAXIMUS

Maximus, you are aptly named, for you represent
    the kinds of excellence left and right both
join to admire—your individual merit, a match
    for your noble birth as one of the Fabii.
But do you meanwhile wonder who it is that presumes
    thus to address you, of what merit or name?
Alas! What can I do? I can see your eyes narrow,
    your jaw set into sternness, and your heart
harden as you look to the signature. I admit
    the justice of what you do, for I deserve
even a worse punishment than what I was given
    (and that has damned near killed me). I live among
enemies, in the midst of dangers—as if my exile
    were not merely from Rome but civilization
itself, from order and peace. The hostile tribesmen here
    don't know such words or have occasion to use them.
These are the people for whom an arrow isn't enough
    unless it has been dipped in viper's venom.
With these in their quivers, they ride before our garrison's walls
    on scrawny ponies, like wolves at a sheepfold.
We never relax here; our strung bows are never
    relaxed. The town's distinctive architectural

feature is roofs that bristle with incoming arrows to make
      the buildings resemble so many porcupines.
The terrain, meanwhile, is bleak, its horizontals severe
      and unrelieved by any tree. The climate
is also severe, the seasons' round a change of winters:
      deeper, milder, wet, less wet, but always
cold, dank, and dismal. This is my fourth year here,
      and the seasons of my soul have accommodated
and are mostly damp, for my weeping is only interrupted
      by lethargy, or stupor. Niobe's tears
ended at last when the gods turned her into stone,
      cool, hard, and insensible. I envy
her, or Phaëthon's sisters, the Heliads, who were changed,
      even as they wailed his name, into poplars,
solid, stolid. To turn into stone or wood, I should brave
      Medusa herself, but her herpetological hairpiece
would be unremarkable here and probably ineffective.
      My model, I fear, is Tityus, whose liver,
always growing, was always unconsumed, deathless
      but only so that it could be always dying.
My dreams are tortures, horrors that mimic the real dangers
      I live with every day, or else oases
that turn out to be mirages. I toss and writhe to avoid
      Sarmatian arrows, or try to free my wrists
from a captor's bonds; or else I see the Roman Forum
      solid and then dissolving with you, my friends,
and my dear wife distorted, disappearing, the wounds
      of our separation torn open again
tender and welling blood as they were on the first day.
      Thus, by day and then by night, I suffer
without even the hope of any respite but death,
      which I should welcome, except that I hate the prospect
of being buried here, of having Sarmatian earth's
      cheap and scratchy blanket cover my bones.

My only hope of relief is great Augustus, by whose
     mercy I have lived thus far and from whom
a kindness may yet transport me, a favorable current
     to carry the wreck of my life to some safe haven
or sheltered cove. For years I have kept that hope alive—
     its embers glowed in my heart's hearth. But the cold
winds wail outside my hut, my destiny's keening
     monotone, and I freeze in despair and fear
and stare at this earthen floor, unable to look for better
     times in a better place. Trapped, I turn
to you, to appeal to your generous heart. What can you do?
     With your impressive eloquence, your stature,
you might work the miracle, moderating for me
     these agonies. I appeal to your known weakness,
your fondness for difficult cases. Mine's as tough as you'll get—
     but not hopeless if Maximus be spokesman!
Only let Caesar know what it is like out here,
     make some allusion to how severely I suffer,
and he may be surprised. Great matters engross him,
     and he can't notice trivial details
in which I am lost, perhaps misfiled and then forgotten . . .
     What can he know of the Tomitae? Why would he
care where the Getan regions are or about their rigors?
     Why would any Roman be interested
in Sauromatian customs or the odd rites of passage
     the Iazyges follow . . . They don't come up often
as subjects of conversation at dinner parties or even
     smokers and stags. Still, you might describe,
by way of making a joke, how when the Danube freezes,
     the tribesmen's horses' hooves ring out on the ice
and we cower here behind our pitiful wattled walls.
     They don't know what Rome is, respect, or fear it.
All they know is hunger, thirst, and the recklessness
     those two always spawn. If Caesar had known

what it was like here, he wouldn't have let his finger
     light on the dot that represents this outland
on the big map on his wall. He couldn't have wanted me
     or any Roman citizen taken captive
by these barbarous tribes. He wouldn't have spared my life.
     A nod of his head, and I'd have been put to death,
but that's not what he had in mind. Nor can this be.
     Or even if it was, years have gone by,
and he may have relented. What I then forced him to
     may no longer compel. His own spirit,
generous to a fault, may only wait some prompting
     from someone like you, Maximus. Let him be
his best self! The pity of my condition here,
     your eloquence, his mercy . . . must combine
to some effect, not for my happiness, but merely
     a diminution of my misery, safety—
just the just sadness of the exile to which I have been
     consigned. Even as I write, some dirty
Getan hones his dagger's curved blade. The god
     didn't mean for my throat to be cut that way.
I plead with you: plead in my behalf, keep
     my ashes from being scattered across the steppes
of Asia. If there is life after death, my spirit
     must not roam these wastes or howl along
endlessly with wind's weird ululation here!
     Does my sad story move you in any way?
If so, then you can be the lever by which the larger
     heart of Caesar is also moved. Your voice
can amplify my own and speak for me as you have
     spoken before for the helpless and the hopeless.
What hero's heart is so hard as not to soften
     at your honeyed tongue? And you won't be addressing
a villain. There's no Theromedon feeding his pet lions
     on human flesh, but a decent, gentle prince

slow to anger, quick to reward, and sorry whenever
    he's forced to play the disciplinary father.
Indulgent, he prefers the threat of force to the real
    use of the thunderbolt his reluctant hand
sometimes looses. The question I beg you to put to him
    is modest indeed—that he might moderate
the terms of my exile and let me live in a less remote,
    less god-forsaken spot. I used to sit
not so far from the head of the table in your house,
    and it wasn't a matter then of life or death
how far away I was. I starve here, I perish
    of thirst, who offered the song at your wedding feast
and led the procession of burning torches to the chamber
    to which you and your bride later withdrew . . .
Do you and Marcia ever remember that night or read
    those verses again I wrote for that occasion?
Think of that! Think how my wife and your own
    are relatives—and not so distant! And speak
for her who asserts a familial claim you cannot deny
    and still maintain your honor. Yes, I know
how I am beyond all sense of shame as I cling to my wife's
    skirts as she in turn clings to the hem
of your toga. And tears run down our faces as we
    beg you to beg Caesar. You can soften
his heart, let him imagine the tomb in which I rot
    out here, and let him let it be less remote.

I, 3   To Rufinus

Greetings from Tomis! It's Naso, dropping a cheery line,
    your old friend—that is if so wretched a man

can be anyone's old friend. I got your letter and took
     consolation, your offer of aid and hope
balm to my heart. Philoctetes himself could not
     have been better soothed by the art of Machaon
than I was by your hearty words of encouragement. Weak,
     at the last raveling end of my rope, I
revived as a dying man will sometimes rally a little
     at a drop of wine some friend helps him get down,
holding the cup up to his all but lifeless lips.
     I rally but do not heal; I am not whole.
The woe you assuage is bilge in a leaky and foundering boat.
     You bail but the flood continues, the water rising.
So it is with me. Perhaps in time a scar
     may form and the raw wound no longer throb
at even the gentlest touch. It's not the physician's fault.
     Some diseases defy the powers of doctors,
the shrewder of whom know when they ought to turn away—
     as from the fellow who's coughing up blood.
Not even a consult with Aesculapius can do
     much for him. Or the man on the battlefield
whose wound is to the heart—they don't waste precious time
     on him but turn to the next case they perhaps
can help to live. For gout, for dropsy, for certain sorrows
     there's nothing that can be done but wring the hands
and counsel patience: "In time you may grow accustomed to it;
     or perhaps it will get better; or you may die
of this or of something else; but either way, there's a likely
     end to it." The patient becomes inured,
learns the stoic's trick of separating himself
     from whatever it is that's eating away at his
own guts. I've done it myself, putting on the old
     emotional armor and clanking bravely about
like any tough Roman should. But the very designation
     stabs me afresh, undoes me, my patriotism

turning me womanish weak. Ulysses kept up his courage
    imagining Ithacan smoke that coiled up into
the bowl of the sky that was over his head too. But I
    can draw no strength even from such a fancy,
knowing how it isn't merely distance that keeps me
    far from home. Let us agree that Rome
is the best of all possible places and this the worst of all
    frozen and dreadful outlands. Nevertheless,
the Scythian in Rome is blind to that city's splendors.
    preferring these barren, blasted steppes I hate
but to which he longs unreasonably—incredibly—to return
    as Philomela, snug in her cage, longs
for the open fields and forests in which to sing, as bullocks
    seek their familiar pastures, or lions their old
lairs . . . And you would think to wean my heart
    of its longing to go home again, to fit,
to be where I belong. If you and your kin were less
    dear to my heart, it might take more comfort
from what you write—that I am a part of all mankind,
    that my poet's citizenship is universal.
But it isn't so. The earth out here has hidden itself
    as if in shame under the permafrost
and constant snows. The fields, untilled, produce nothing
    nor do the vines and trees on the naked hills.
Even the sea is sunless and gray, whipped by the winds'
    frenzies. Mankind has not touched this place,
gentled or tamed it. Just to hang on here is more
    than one can imagine. Enemies harass us
on all sides, Bistonian spears and Sarmatian arrows
    busy the air like gnats . . . Buck up, you say?
How can I think of it? Your good examples only
    depress me! Noble Rutilius chose exile.
True enough, but to Smyrna! A real place, a civilized
    city! I dream of Smyrna and its comforts!

Diogenes bore his exile well—but consider where:
    in Attica! And Themistocles went only
to Argos. And Aristides did his time in Sparta.
    Patroclus fled to the Thessaly of Achilles.
And Jason, Cadmus, Tydeus, and Teucer, where did they
    all go? But look where I am and what
I have to bear who am hardly one of those old heroes
    but only Ovid, whose little courage is long
spent, and I am bankrupt, broke, broken. You try
    to save me, but it can't be done. I'm grateful
for your attentions, but know my own case better than any
    doctor. The signs and symptoms are not subtle.
If there were any remedy, doctrine or herbal cure,
    I'm sure your ministrations would be helpful.
But I am too far gone, desperate, and hope itself
    is only a mockery now, another wound
you cannot mean to inflict. And I am not ungrateful,
    but only beyond help. Hard to imagine,
but there it is, and I pray you never have the occasion
    to come to understand what I'm talking about.
You are a decent fellow, you always were, and your letter
    meant well, as it meant much to receive it.
I turn my face to the wall and try to hide my tears
    as I thank you, truly, for all your kind intentions.

I, 4   To His Wife

I'm falling apart, ramshackle, dilapidating to ruin,
    cracks crazing what's left of my façade.
In any decent neighborhood, I should be a disgrace.
    If you could see me now, you wouldn't know me,

couldn't pick me out from a line-up of local geezers
　　　randomly rounded up on these muddy streets.
Age will do that, even in Rome—but the passage of time
　　　measures its assaults as a rule, and I
invoke that rule—count blows instead of years,
　　　and thus figure myself older than Nestor.
You've seen in the fields how even the strength of bullocks
　　　breaks with the toil of the plow. The field itself,
if it isn't given a rest and left to lie fallow, yields
　　　less and less, exhausted. Or back in the city,
the trainer knows his horses don't have a hope of winning
　　　if they race too often. And ships, unless they're hauled
into fresh water and scraped, turn sluggish, even break up.
　　　Enough? I agree. My point exactly. I'm old
before my time with this disproportionate series of woes.
　　　When Jason came in the Argo to this malign
strand, he'd been sent by Pelias, the ripple of whose name
　　　carried no farther than Thessaly; Augustus
can batter this beach and flood it, a terrible tidal wave.
　　　Jason came about half as far as I,
and wasn't alone. I didn't have any crew or companions
　　　like Tiphys, the pilot, or Phineus as guides.
Nor did I have Minerva and Juno, the queen of heaven,
　　　protecting me as their pet, defending my life.
Cupid came to his aid, that scamp! (And what has he done
　　　for me, after what I did for him? It isn't
fair!) But worst and hardest to bear is the end of the story:
　　　Jason went back, reached home again, but I
despair, can no longer imagine setting my foot upon
　　　the deck of a ship that will take me away from here.
I'm going to die here, unless the wrath of the god
　　　eases. There's nothing for it, no way out.
My dear wife, my hand trembles to write the words,
　　　but we've known it a long time in our mute bones.

And you? Your burden of cares is only slightly less
  than mine—but it wrings my heart to imagine them.
Your hair must be different now, has grayed perhaps at the
              temples,
  but I rather suppose it feels the same and smells
the way it did. I yearn to touch it, to stroke it again,
  to kiss it as I used to do. I yearn
to take you in my arms again and soothe the hurts
  I've caused, myself, the traces of which are all
badges of merit, decorations of highest honor.
  It is your love for me that has distressed
your beauty, turning it noble, turning your face holy.
  To touch the lines on your cheek with my fingertips
would be the miracle cure I still can dream about.
  Our tears would spring forth the way freshets arise
at holy places, and pilgrims would come with their little phials.
  It's all I live for—to sit with you and talk
the way we used to do about the impossible years
  that separated us, the trials we've passed.
I pray to the Caesars to pity our plight, to let it happen.
  The dawn of that glorious day waits to be born.

I, 5   TO MAXIMUS

Not the last on your list of friends (although it's not
  this year's list, I confess), still you remember
Naso? These are his words on the page before you. For old
  times' sake, he imposes on Maximus: Read!
Graceless, possibly dull, excessively earnest surely,
  I'm not the fancy Dan you used to know.

Use it or lose it, the athletes say, meaning their bodies,
       but that's not all that goes flabby if you don't
keep it working. Even water that's left to stand
       turns cloudy or scummy. My brain is like that.
These pitifully awkward lines are costing me effort, my
       hand balking at every word. It's heavy
going, uninspired . . . The muse's regular route
       does not extend this far. What would she offer
to Getae, or they to her but dumb puzzled stares?
       I read over these couplets and see their faults—
they want to be improved or stricken out. I let them
       stand, not having the heart to amend what my head
has already botched. My craftsman's pride is gone with the rest
       of my self-esteem. A broken man, I can't
mend defective verses. The quill in my hand won't
       fly and can't remember having done so
in another life. The decent plowman spares the ox
       whose neck the yoke has galled. I should do as much
for myself. Why not? It isn't greed that keeps me going
       (or call it, rather the profit motive). There's no
profit in any of this. My work has brought me only
       catastrophic loss. At parties people
used to ask me why I wrote. They weren't nasty
       or mean but merely curious. Now I wonder
whether it isn't a kind of madness, whether they weren't
       right to question what the point might be.
Habit? A way of thinking about one's life? The wounded
       gladiator swears to forsake the arena,
but heals and his memory fails him or maybe his mind.
       (How smart is your average gladiator?) The sailor
who swims ashore from the wreck is sure to go back to sea,
       having no idea what else to do with himself.
I'm no smarter than they are, and I go back to the altar
       of the cruel goddess I wish I'd never addressed.

The only alternative I can see is inanition—
    idleness, which is death. Gambling? Drink?
Oblivion's all right, but sooner or later one wakes,
    one gets through the worst of the hangover and then
there's the rest of the day, yawning like some mythical monster.
    What can I feed it? I've thought of working out,
building my body up, joining the civil guard,
    turning burly, going native . . . A joke!
I'm not the type. My body rebels at my mind's absurd
    thought and I'm left with the old useless pursuit.
But what is more useful than this art that has no use?
    It isn't a mere means but an end in itself!
What it can nevertheless accomplish is amazing:
    I can forget for minutes at a time
my miseries here—no mean yield for these stony fields.
    Back in Rome, you labor for fame, burn
your lamp at night in the hope of winning approval. I
    am freed of all that nonsense. Who out here
would approve? Some Getan who takes his shoe off to count
    to eleven? I'm freed of envy as well. Whom
should I envy here? I can call myself the voice of the mouth
    of the Danube. Here, to call oneself a poet
is amazing, the mere intention enough to distinguish
    a votary of the Muse, who takes what she gets
or gets nothing—as I have learned from my own sad case.
    My books travel . . . at least in theory they do.
It's hard to believe that it works in actual practice, that these
    flimsy scrolls can stretch to span the sky
from here as far as the Quirinal. Still, let us suppose
    that these words may be read, months or years
from now in a civilized villa, and even suppose they please,
    move or amuse . . . what can it matter to me?
What would it mean to you if it could be demonstrated
    that someone in the Sudan were reading you now,

or a fan in Sri Lanka were nodding his head in wonder
    at how you'd expressed his own deepest self?
Or look even further, upwards . . . Imagine the Pleiades
    populated, civilized, and assume
intelligent admiration for all the work you've done.
    What earthly good is it going to do you? And I
know my defects, which makes it hard to imagine even
    that theoretical triumph. I get what I
deserve in art as well as in what we still call real
    life, which is nothing, oblivion's acrid dust.
Your eyes, glazed with boredom, figure the whole story—
    my memory's exile, ignominy, and death.

I, 6 To Graecinus

On duty at some remote post, you didn't hear
    the news of my disaster for months, but then,
tough as you think you are, you would have been deeply grieved.
    Your friends all see through you, know your pose
of the tough campaigner is just that. Your heart is gentle,
    your spirit almost finical. You detest
cruelty. A soldier, you have devoted yourself
    to keeping the peace, which is what they always claim.
Mostly it's an empty boast, but not with you,
    devoted as you are to life's graces,
a connoisseur, a patron of the arts. When it happened, I
    thought of you—or did when I could think,
when the first shock had worn off, and my brain began
    groping through the thick smoke. I thought
of my absent friend whose courage and counsel I so much needed,
    generous as you've always been with support

of every kind to those in great need. And now,
    even at this late date and from this awful
distance, you can still supply much of that comfort—
    inspiriting words to an old friend who was more
foolish than wicked. Believe me, what I set down is the truth.
    I'd tell you the whole story, but for the fear
of opening old wounds. The scars are ugly enough
    and the flesh there is still tender. Enough
that I confess a fault that was not a crime—a mistake
    (or is every mistake that offends the gods a crime?).
I haven't yet abandoned all hope of mollification
    of the punishment I endure. Or say that goddess
has not abandoned me. She's the only one we have
    in this god-forsaken spot. The chain-gang slave
clings to Hope. And the shipwrecked sailor, weary, his arms
    heavy as lead, and no land anywhere,
swims another stroke and another, at Hope's command.
    The patient of whom doctors have all despaired,
whose pulse is fluttering, still clings with strength to Hope.
    To the convict in his dark cell or hanging
in agony on his cross she ministers with her mercy.
    To how many men who have already tied the noose
and picked out a sturdy ceiling beam has she come to stay them
    from that last terrible step into the thin
air? And I too had been thinking, could see it clearly,
    could already feel myself falling on my
sword, when she rebuked me, asking, "What are you doing?
    Shed your tears, which may soften a prince's heart,
but not your life's blood!" I may not deserve her tender
    attentions, but Hope persists—of some improvement,
which can only come, I know, from another god's kindness.
    Speak to him Graecinus, add your voice
to my annoying supplication, or I will languish,
    die, and be covered over with the sand

on this barren shingle. Pigeons will sooner leave their dove-cotes,
    the wild beasts quit their shaded forest glades,
cattle their meadows, or gulls their marshy inlets, than you
    will abandon your old friends. Graecinus, my blessings!

I, 7   To Messalinus

The breath of the greeting I send dies and the words resolve
    to curious squiggles the fierce Getae fear
for their possible magical powers. For once, they are quite right!
    It is a kind of magic that from this outpost
at the end of the world, my words can fly back to Rome from
                                         your old
    friend—Naso! (What other friend could you have
at such a remove? None, I pray. And that you
    may never yourself behold a shaggy Getan
face—even in zoos, which is where they belong.) It's enough
    that I should report on the flora and fauna of this
ice palace where Scythian arrows score the skies
    like flocks of skinny birds. War and Cold
are the savage gods of this otherwise godless and terrible place.
    What is there here for any self-respecting
god to preside over? Abundant crops? Fruits?
    Nothing but savage empty space. I blink,
but it doesn't go away. Let me be the only friend
    or acquaintance of yours to suffer these exotic
torments . . . Or do I presume? Would you rather deny me?
    Is that another pill I have to swallow?
Say, if you must, that I lie. The Caesars themselves put up
    with such professions of intimacy from people

they can't remember ever having set eyes on. Take it
    as a kind of praise, or else an expression of my
naked need, deserving of some compassion. Your father
    did not deny having known me. He was my patron,
and I was your brother in grief when he died. You, your brother,
    and I wept tears together to make a bond
as thick as that of the blood of Atreus' sons. You must
    remember the verses—mine—at the funeral rite.
My love for your house is such that I give you leave to deny
    ever having met me, if there should be taint
or even inconvenience in this display of your name
    at the top of one of these letters. But better say
what's true—that you had no power over your old friend,
    could not keep him out of trouble, and therefore are not
responsible for the mess he's made of his life, his folly—
    which is what Caesar himself called it, who sees
all things. He showed me mercy, loosed the smallest
    thunderbolt in his quiver upon my head.
I have kept life, my estate, my citizenship and the hope
    of return someday. All that I need is for you
to voice a prayer to assuage the imperial anger.
    It was a disaster. Even a glancing blow
from the mighty Jove will produce a terrible wound. Achilles,
    even if he restrained his mighty arm
when he threw his ash spear, would still do dreadful damage.
    That I am still alive is a kind of credential
I do not blush to use, almost a badge of honor.
    I flash it like an invitation at your
doorkeeper. And when he sends to inquire whether
    I should be turned away or allowed inside,
don't pretend you don't know me. I've been your guest
    from time to time, and frequently at your brother's
house—which gives me a small claim on the household god
    you share and whose protection I have enjoyed.

Remote? Even absurd? Surely, but isn't it also
 flattering to be asked to intervene?
Noblesse oblige! It's what you have to put up with. It comes
 with the territory. That you are a public figure,
famous for your good deeds, is not such a terrible fate,
 if you'll allow me to say so. It costs, of course,
but you can afford it! You grumble from time to time, but you also
 pride yourself on being able to bear it,
on giving more than you get. And I say, Hallelujah!
 and Amen, brother! I'll say whatever you like—
in a ghostly voice you'd hardly recognize. For my woes,
 weep, or if you believe, as I have come
myself to believe, that they're all my own doing, then weep
 at my foolishness in having deserved such woes.

I, 8   To Severus

Friend, colleague, companion, accept a warm greeting
 from your faithful Naso. But be careful! Do not
reply in the usual way, asking me how I am.
 You don't want to hear. If I were to answer that question
you'd be reduced to tears, and I should weep along with you.
 But skip, as they say, to the chase. The shortest version
is that my diet of hardship is seasoned with danger. My exile
 is also a kind of conscription. Out here the distinction
blurs in the face of the savage Getan raiders who don't
 distinguish except between what they will kill for food
and what they kill for sport. Grant, therefore, indulgence
 to the verses you now read, as if they'd been written
on a battlefield, which doesn't stretch by much the truth.
 Not far from here is an old fortified town

Aegisos, the Caspian founded and named after himself.
    It's high and hard to get to. Still, the Getae
took it in a sneak attack. The King of Thrace
    thereafter took it back with a levy of troops
that included some from the garrison here. They say
    it was an abattoir more than a battle,
and the gutters ran red with human blood. And we
    rejoiced to hear it! We? I, Ovid,
your gentle friend, was glad! My spirit, too, is conscripted,
    which gives a wholly different dimension to griefs
that beggar description. Such changes are commonplace
    here along the bleak banks of the Danube—
which cannot be much different from those of the dismal Styx.
    Since we last met, the Pleiades have risen
four times in the heavens to signal as many autumns.
    You imagine me here longing for city pleasures,
as of course I do, but what I miss even more sorely
    are the friends from whom I am separated—you,
a few others, my daughter, my dear wife. In dreams
    I see myself at home, can touch the walls,
can walk from my door along familiar streets I loved—
    but not enough. My eyes are sharper now
than they were. I should have stared harder and memorized
    each portico, each bush and flowering shrub.
Like a blind man I rub my fists in my dark sockets
    to make those stars come by whose faint light
I might see the Campo, its green lawn, the pretty pools,
    the grace and strength of the aqueduct of Virgo . . .
And delights of country living? I can already hear
    your counter argument, that surely they
must offer themselves still. I must remember the tilled
    fields and their earthy smells, or the pine-clad hills
past which the Clodian Way and Flaminian Way wind
    like ribbons a giant has strewn on the countryside.

I used to entertain my guests who came to the country,
     would show off in my garden plants I had tended
with my own hands, watering, weeding, pruning, and plucking
     their fruits . . . And I could do that here, you say. Why not?
Even an exile can have his little plot, or his flock
     of goats to tend, for the solace of the familiar.
You see me on a gentle bluff, leaning on my crook,
     and counting my sheep. Or following my bullock
as I plow the furrow in which I will sow the seeds
     from my gentleman farmer's catalogue, and cursing
in the Getic language they're trained to (and priding myself
     in having learned those words). But it's all wrong,
can't happen. There's nothing like that here. We can't
     hoe a garden wearing armor, and mustn't ever
venture beyond the walls without that armor. You can't
     imagine what it's like here, and I rejoice
with my whole heart that you cannot. Strolling the Campo
     avoiding the sun by moving along the wall
or portico of some beautiful temple, or sitting
     in an Umbrian garden beneath an arbor and sipping punch,
you simply cannot grasp it. You may think of me, wish
     that Caesar might abate his wrath and allow
me to visit you there . . . But it's too much to ask. Better
     wish more modestly, furling your prayer's sail.
All I want is a less remote, less dangerous place
     in which to weep and repent in safety and peace.

I, 9   TO MAXIMUS

I read your letter with news of the death of Celsus, blurred
     with my tears, then spotted, and then soggy.

If you'll forgive my rudeness in saying so, it's the worst
     letter I've had since I've been here, the one I read
with the most unwilling eyes. I pray it may have no rival
     for that distinction. Celsus' image remains
as clear in my mind as if he were here, before me—my love
     having learned to leap enormous distances. I
can see him smile, can hear him laughing aloud, but most
     remember how, on that worst day of my life,
his steadiness was there beside me, his comfort and faith.
     I saw him weep as if for his own brother's
disaster. He had no obligation, could just as well
     have made himself scarce as so many others did.
But he was there, consoling, embracing, his copious tears
     commingled with mine. And he was the one who stayed
my desperate hand that was ready to make an end to it then
     and there. "Live!" he commanded. "There's still hope!"
And he told me what you could do for me. "Maximus loves you.
     He and his brother will beg Caesar to lighten
your burden of pain," he said, with his lips at my ear, and I
     listened and lived. Maximus, for his sake
as much as my own, speak to Caesar, come to my aid!
     See that the last words I heard from him
are more than vanities. He revered your house and knew
     that I did, too—not for your wealth or power
but for the even rarer gift of personal honor.
     It is only right that I should weep for Celsus,
repaying now a part of my debt of that river of tears
     he shed for me years ago. It is only
right that I should fashion these funerary verses
     if not for him at least for his memory's sake,
but also for those of us whose lives his life continues
     to grace. And those who are not yet born may read
the name and imagine what he was—a noble vessel
     of all the virtues whose fame reached even here
to this desperate end of the earth. I remember he promised

he might surprise me, make the journey, pay
a visit, and in his elaborate daydream he mentioned you,
    Maximus, our friend, who might arrange permission.
It didn't happen. And won't. And here where the mother lode
    of grief is everywhere underfoot, I mine
my sorrows to make this dirge, refine it and give it shape—
    who cannot follow the corpse as I ought to have done,
or stand watch as the door of the tomb is sealed shut.
    Farewell, my friend. I am at least consoled
to hear the report that Maximus was there, presiding over
    your last rites and pouring out the fragrant
balsam onto your bosom. In his grief he mingled
    the unguents with his own hot tears as he
lay your bones to rest. In the sacred ground, he observed,
    I am sure, every piety and discharged
the last debt a friend can pay to a dead companion—
    and I beg him in your name to show to me, another
departed—almost dead—friend, the same degree
    of attention, observing the scruples of friendship and honor.

I, 10   To Flaccus

A salutation from Naso—but one must wonder how
    from such insalubriousness as plagues me
I can send a *Health* to anyone. Vitiated,
    dull, and torpid, I languish. I'm not in pain,
don't burn with fever or shake with chills, and my heart
    beats in a more or less regular way. But I
have no appetite. Food tastes like straw. I eat
    but only from habit. Meals are an awful bore,
and the straw, once I've managed to get it down, turns into

bricks in my stomach. I'm not just a picky eater—
what are the goodies here for a dainty fellow to crave?
    I swear it's not that. Let my enemies all
feel as I do about food and drink, and then claim
    the sentence Caesar laid on me was lenient.
I waste away. Aside from the dietary problem,
    I'm also having trouble sleeping at night,
toss and turn, or drift off to terrible dreams from which
    I wrench myself awake, afraid, exhausted,
and more worn out than I was when I first crawled into bed.
    At home, when people rouse from a nightmare, the cure
is to look around at the normal and reassuring world.
    If I look around here, it's another nightmare
every bit as bad as the one my brain had concocted.
    You'd hardly recognize me. I'm a cartoon
of what I used to be—my color's gone, and I look
    like someone has done a bad job at Tussaud's.
It isn't as if I'd been hitting the old wineskin. I'm not
    a lush—you know my habits: my drink of choice
is cold water. And when I was able to taste food
    I never made a pig of myself, not even
with dishes I liked. (And what is there in the Getic cuisine
    to like or even with certainty recognize?)
To the other obvious question, the answer is also, No—
    I haven't been whoring around. Venus does not
offer much in the way of consolation to those
    who suffer from depressions. No, it's the water,
the bad air, the climate, and my real sorrows that weigh
    me down, sapping my body, mind, and spirit.
If it weren't for you and your brother, I couldn't have stood it.
    You are the sight of land to a shattered vessel.
You gave me comfort when others denied me or turned away.
    I beg you, don't give me up—as long as Caesar
persists in his anger. But pray to all the gods you know
    that he may lessen his justifiable wrath.

BOOK II

II, 1   TO GERMANICUS CAESAR

Even to this remote place has the fame of Caesar's
        triumph arrived, where the winds themselves gasp,
panting for breath after so long a journey. News—
        or call it recent history—is a wonder
like fresh fruit here. And good news? We hardly
        know how to deal with it. Clouds in the sky part;
sunshine pours down; we all blink in wonder
        and rub our eyes—that all along the sky
was blue . . . Imagine that! It's as if I'd cheated my fate,
        for it wasn't Caesar's intention that I should enjoy
happy times out here. But this particular pleasure
        he may not begrudge my sharing. The gods command
one and all on feast days to lay their sorrows aside.
        But even were it expressly forbidden to me,
still I should rejoice, my heart gladdened by your
        news. The rains pour down, and in with the crops,
weeds and burs flourish. Useless weed though I be,
        I drink the life-giving moisture and offer thanks
to the bountiful god. And the glory of Caesar's house cannot
        be contained or restrained, but carries even
here to the land of the Getae. Fame, tireless, brings
        splendid tales of the triumph—how every *gens*
was assembled to look on the leader's face, how the vast walls
        could scarcely contain the throng of Rome's guests.
The story is that it rained for days, and then, that morning,
        the sun broke through to burnish the gleaming city.
Out here we treasure each distinct glint, as the glimpses
        of one in the jostling crowd—of how the victor
honors the people of Rome and bestows gifts on his chosen
        heroes; how he sprinkles the sacred hearth
with incense; how he dons the ceremonial vestments,
        embroidered and trimmed; and how the very streets

he walks on acquire the look of those richly worked goods,
    first bedecked and then dyed with the roses
the adoring throng throws at his feet. And they all applaud,
    and men wave the placards with pictures of towns
you took and the rivers and forests you crossed, and all the prizes,
    glittering gold. And then in their slow procession,
the chieftains you conquered come, the chains on their
                                    necks clanking—
    a long line in numbers not only impressive
but frightening too. Enough to have been, all by themselves,
    a host to intimidate pacific souls.
And most of these you have pardoned—even Bato, the chief
    of all their chieftains. (My heart raced when I heard
that piece of news, for if there can be such abundant mercy
    to such as him, then what can I not allow
my tired hopes to imagine from the same generous source?)
    But back to your parade! Here come the models of towns,
the floats of their rude forts, their walls and their arms unable
    to withstand your fierce assault! And there they go,
leaving behind the idea of your valor's achievement, which we
    even here can conceive. The prayers of poets
are not, after all, worthless; the god understands how
    our eulogies are amber preserving forever
delicate features that otherwise fade of even our greatest
    sons. Your father shall bask in his son's honors,
rejoice in the rich return, the usufruct of the gifts
    with which he endowed you. Some day he shall watch
as you ascend the Capitoline Hill in the last
    of your series of triumphs, and I shall perhaps be there
to sing your song of praise—assuming of course that my blood
    has not been spilled by a Getan sword or poisoned
by a Scythian arrowhead. Let us hope not! Courage!
    Faith! It may yet happen, and I shall be
proud for having foretold how it would one day befall.
    I live for that day, Germanicus, and I pray

to see you take the laurel just as I'm writing it here—
    a splendid dream come double-splendidly true!

II, 2   To Messalinus

One who, from his earliest years, has venerated your house
    sends from the sinister shore of the Pontus greetings.
From me, Naso, who formerly tendered them face to face . . .
    Do not wrinkle yours or this poor paper,
but, I beg you, persevere. Don't banish my words.
    My verses are still, in the city's limits, licit.
I never thought of piling Pelion onto Ossa
    to make a step-stool on which to touch,
in Enceladus' madness, the stars. Overthrowing the gods
    is not my cup of tea. I never presumed
like Diomedes to strike at gods with an ash spear.
    My misdemeanor was grave enough to undo me
but only me. It's not, I promise you, sir, contagious.
    To "Timid," I plead guilty, also to "Stupid."
I'll answer to those words as if they were pet names—
    they're less insulting than what I call myself.
I agree with your harshest judgment that I deserved what I got,
    and you have been quite correct to ignore my pleas.
Such is your devotion to Augustus and his house,
    that when any of them is injured, you are too.
I write this having little to fear even from your
    anger—what can you do worse than already
has been done? Desperate, I turn to you rather for good.
    It sometimes happens. Look to the old stories,
of Ulysses' shipmate, for instance, Achaemenides whom
    Aeneas, a Trojan, rescued from Sicily's beaches.

Or think of Telephus, chief of the Mysians. He was a Trojan,
    but the curative rust for his wound came from Achilles'
Greek spear. It turns out that way, sometimes. A sinner
    can apply to the very god whom he has offended.
Dangerous, surely, but desperate cases require strong
    measures for their remedies. Uttermost grief
has at least the assurance of nothing worse to fear.
    The sailor going down in the foaming maelstrom
will clutch at the dangerous rocks, reach out to grasp at thorns.
    An exhausted bird, fleeing the savage raptor,
will alight at last in the human habitation she dreads
    only slightly less, and the running doe
will try to hide from the baying hounds in the hunter's barn.
    Such things happen, curious, teasing with meaning—
and I beg you, in that spirit to consider my plea, my tears,
    my all but holy hopelessness. Do not
shut your doors, or your ears against me, but carry my words
    higher on to the god both of us worship.
I'm a dying man. Already, I feel the fatal chill's
    cold, clammy embrace. My only hope
is of you. Not from me but from weakness itself the cry
    sounds in your ear—speak for it to the Prince
whose love for you has made you a power in Rome. How better
    to show what it is in that power to do? In you
and your brother both, the eloquent tongue of your father has
                     found
    its remarkable heirs. To you, therefore, I turn
not for defense—I admit my guilt to you and the world—
    but for help. Palliation. Mercy! We shall not dwell
on what I did. The wound is past all ministration
    and still smarts at the touch. Better to leave it
alone. I only wish it were in my power to bury
    my own ashes. Instead, start from the sentence
your friend pronounced upon me, accepting no more and no less
    than what he intended for me. Still you can speak,

can plead that I may enjoy the life he allowed me. Look
    to a pleasant moment, observe the famous features,
and pick a time when he is serene, when the empire's peace
    shows in his face. Ask him then (or beg him)
not to let me be prey to some Getan savage, to grant
    a peaceful land for my exile that still would be
an exile from home and Rome. It stands to reason that this
    is a good time for petitions: Caesar is well,
and all is well with Rome; Caesar's consort thrives;
    his son, Tiberius, pushes our territory's
borders and his own fame to ever greater reaches;
    Germanicus and Drusus fulfill in abundant
measure the great demands of their noble birth; the distaff
    side of the house in no way lacks in honor,
gifts, or health; the armies send back reports of success
    in Pannonia, and Dalmatia; Illyria too
submits her head to Caesar's foot. We have heard the news
    of Tiberius' triumph for his great victory there.
We are told Tiberius' sons were with you and your brother
    as he advanced, like Castor and Pollux—that Julius
contemplates from his shrine in the facing temple. To this
    blessed and happy family, Messalinus
stands close, and for them he rejoices. Nobody else
    has better reason to do so or closer ties.
I envy you your delight in witnessing these parades
    and ceremonies I only dream of here.
I see it all, vivid and clear, but then some rude
    noise wakes me. I startle. Abruptly, Caesar's
features give way to a caricature's, to a barely human
    party mask that's a Sauromatian face.
I go to the window and see instead of the Forum some
    bare heath, its ground churned and bloody.
Even the harbor's frozen water writhes in grotesque
    constructions. My eyes sicken and close again—

I only wish my brain was also equipped with a lid.
　　Still, if my words carry, and if my voice
can reach as far as Rome and you hear my words, repeat them,
　　let your influence work to my benefit, change
this *mise en scène,* I pray you. In the name of your famous father
　　whose shade must still be eloquent and persuasive,
in your brother's name as well, and in that of every guest
　　with whom I enjoyed a place at your generous table—
in all those names I implore you, do what you can for me
　　and my wasted talent that I may yet employ it
in such a way as to merit your old words of praise.
　　Speak for me to Caesar. On my life,
I promise nothing I do in the time of it that remains
　　shall give you cause to regret your help. I honor
your house and wish its occupants well. May the Caesars continue
　　their favors—and may one of those be through you
to me, however much cause I've given for anger, that he
　　may remove me from Scythian wastes that are less a landscape
than a grand guignol backdrop. I know it's a lot to ask
　　of you and Caesar, but virtue despises easy
objectives. My thanks and praise will be the only employment
　　I'll have in those easier days. I do not send you
to speak to a Polyphemus in one of Aetna's caverns
　　or address a cannibal king like Antiphates,
but a lenient father ready to pardon any offense.
　　He thunders, but then the lightning is often withheld.
He'll make his harsh decisions, but sadly—as in my case,
　　where the fault outweighed his mercy. I cannot throw
myself at his feet from here. You be my priest and carry
　　my prayers adding your own—if you think the time
auspicious. (Forgive me, my nerve is gone—I'm a shipwrecked
　　　　　　　　　　　　　　　　　　　　　　　　　　sailor
　　who fears the waves that separate him from home.)

II, 3   TO MAXIMUS

I write your name, observing, as I must have done before,
 it's a soubriquet for your virtue and generous spirit.
Maximus, you're immense! It was by no means a mean
 achievement to have lived up to your name and the great
demands of your noble birth—and you have, as I can attest,
 the unfortunate friend whom a lesser would have already
disowned. I shouldn't like to say how many have done
 exactly that. It's the terrible times. Or else
it has always been this way, though neither of us suspected
 how friendship is mostly a mask, a thin veneer
beneath which is the sordid calculation of profit,
 the balance of gains and costs. Honor? It doesn't
figure, or loyalty. Those are words for the rhetoricians
 schoolboys copy into their books. Where
is the pride in a good deed done for its own sake?
 You can stop scores of men, or hundreds—thousands—
before you find a one in the Forum who still believes
 in such old-fashioned principles. The rest
will look at you with that pained gaze affliction elicits.
 The temple of friendship's goddess is empty, abandoned,
and the deity now strolls the pavements, a fallen woman.
 So runs the current, or rather the torrent
of these corrupt and vicious times—but you have not
 been carried away. They say that fortune favors
the bold, and it may. But the meek certainly do adore
 those whom fortune has blessed. A turn in one's luck
and they scurry away. I know, having seen their cowardly backs.
 When the winds blew fair and bellied out my sails,
they were a happy crew, but the wind changed and the weather
 turned bad. The waves heaved, and my vessel
wallowed and groaned. And the rats did what rats always do . . .
 It shouldn't have been any surprise, but it was.

And only then did I realize what was truly surprising,
    that some people are different, that two or three
had ignored my disaster and still behaved as if their love
    had been for the abject naked self that was all
that remained of me. And of these, you were the chief, the model
    who did not look to the others' example but set
your own for the decent few to follow, and treated me,
    who had made a mistake, not only with correctness
but kindness too. You think it base to abandon a friend,
    quite out of the question—but the question is always
there, to a drowning man, what the approaching swimmer
    has in mind—to buoy him up a little
or submerge his gasping face for the fun of watching him drown.
    Think of Achilles and what he did for Patroclus
after his death (you may count me, too, as one of the dead);
    or think of Theseus, traveling with his friend,
Pirithous, to the Styx (the dark waters of which
    must be like those of the Black Sea I see here);
and consider Pylades' devotion to his crazy
    friend, Orestes (I'm nearly as crazed myself).
Accept, therefore, praise that is fit for the noblest heroes.
    The worse Fortune treats me, the better you are,
who will not yield to her whims but holds fast to the tiller
    and keeps his course, however battered the vessel
and tattered the sails. You patch, tack, try to make do,
    and by your strength and cunning prevent that wreck
the rest of the world expected. At first, you were justly angered
    and took the view of him whom I'd offended.
And yet I am told that you also groaned in pity to hear
    what kind of fool I'd been and shook your head—
I thank you for that groan, and also for your letter,
    the first I had of comfort, with its brave ray
of hope that the injured god might yet be soothed and moved.
    What in the world could have prompted such an expression

of friendship at such a time but your family's long tradition
    of constancy? Those you have greeted as friends
remain your friends, however their circumstances may change
    as the fickle breath of Fortune blows hot or cold.
Some have become your friends by choice and by elevation;
    for others the title was heritable—as I
was your friend from the day you were born, a noble title
    of which I'm proud. I beamed at you in the cradle
and gave you kisses of welcome you cannot remember now,
    except as a burden, a debt of long standing.
Your famous father, who spoke and wrote the purest Latin
    of anybody in Rome, was the first to urge me
to publish my verses. He was my guide and generous patron.
    Your brother can't remember a time when I didn't
love him and honor him—but we were even closer.
    With you I shared, and to you owed, all things.
When we were last together on Elba, the tears flowed
    from both our sorrowing cheeks as you asked me whether
the reports were true . . . I stammered, unable to choose between
    imposing with my grief and guilt, or compounding
that guilt with the new sin of deceit, and could not answer.
    But my tears flowed all the harder, as if the winter
snows of my heart were melting in the warmth of your

                                  springtime.
    And friend that you are, you knew all and forgave
almost all, but kept your faith with your old companion
    in his time of trial. You comfort me still and help
my wounds to heal. My desperate pleas may yet be answered,
    in which event I shall send you a thousand blessings.
But even if nothing happens, I shall know you have tried
    on my behalf. The blessing will still stand—
only after Caesar's, I pray for your mother's health,
    as you used to do, burning the fragrant incense
at the family shrine's altar, invoking the household gods,
    as fervently as I pray now, to you.

II, 4   TO ATTICUS

With words from the mouth of the Danube, it's Naso, your
                                                old friend . . .
      You remember me? Of course! How can I doubt
the devotion of such an old companion, a good buddy's
      love? How can I judge it except by my own
affectionate feeling? Your face is vivid still in my mind,
      and the good talks we had, our eyes bright
though the lamps guttered. I used to recite my new poems,
      eager for your opinion and your suggestions.
Your approval I took as if it were public acceptance, but tougher
      to get, surer, and therefore all the dearer.
The second prize was even better—when you could not
      delight in what I'd written, you offered me help
I was glad to have, your rough words smoothing mine and buffing
      them to a brighter shine than they'd had before.
Companions we were in the Forum, and side by side we strolled
      the avenues and explored alleys together
went to the theater together, hung out in cafés together,
      the dynamic duo, a mythological pair . . .
And what has happened to us? To you? If someone had told me
      you'd taken to drink—and not just mead but the waters
of Lethe itself—I could not believe that you would forget
      that good talk, those times, the friendship we had.
Impossible! Sooner would long days come in the winter,
      or short days in the summer, with time out of whack,
Sooner would Babylon's weather bureau report cold spells,
      or the one here at the Pontus predict heat waves;
sooner would waxy lilies surpass the roses of Paestum
      in fragrance than you would forget our old friendship.
My fate is black but not so black as that—I am not
      crazy yet. I know who I am. I know
my friends . . . But if I am wrong? I hesitate to think it,
      but wonder which of us will look the worse

if it should turn out that I've been foolish, misplacing my trust.
    For both our sakes, old buddy, keep the faith!

II, 5   TO SALANUS

With a poem constructed of hop-along elegiacs, I,
    Naso, greet Salanus and wish for his health.
Thrive and prosper, and know that I wish you well (and some
    of my wishes may come true—I'm long overdue),
for with your noble nature, you're a rarity in these
    times, a nearly extinct species in need
of protection. Surely you merit my prayers. We knew each other
    only slightly, but still you grieved to hear
the news of my exile, and then grieved afresh when you read
    verses I'd sent from the shore of this black sea
of tears. Your kindness to them was kindness to their author:
    your judgment—that they'd melt the heart of Caesar—
is what I've hoped and lived for, and what I believe will happen
    if these poems could only come into Caesar's
own hands. Your kind remark could be literary
    or another kind of opinion—political, legal,
moral, whatever your soul in its charity declares
    to be right and proper. In any event, I thank you,
and send my blessings from this place you have, yourself,
    denoted "dreadful." As, indeed, it is.
Nowhere in the entire world do they enjoy
    so little as we do here the Peace of Augustus.
What you are now reading is like a report from a war,
    a bulletin scribbled in haste on a battlefield.
That I have earned your approval is only another sign
    of a generous nature: my talent's trickle you treat

like a broad and powerful river. I hold my head high
    to hear such a thing—or anyway less low
than on most days, when I feel my terrible limitations—
    my tongue thick, my hands clumsy, the pen
an unreliable tool in my fingers, as I discovered
    not very long ago when I tried to write
a piece about the recent triumph. Grandeur! The splendor
    wasn't an inspiration. I was scared,
inarticulate, stupid. If you want to be truthful, praise
    my will, my pertinacity and nerve.
In the absence of talent, these come into operation
    and keep one going. Perhaps you've read the poem—
if you want to be kind, that tack is one you can take, may have to
    if you want to extend the courtesies you've shown me
that I don't deserve (but I never did). Your heart is pure,
    a bowl of milk, a field of untrodden snow.
Deserving of admiration, you admire others
    less impressive, as my case demonstrates.
You are Germanicus' friend, have been his companion and tutor,
    your virtues and great talents finding you favor.
You helped him grow into his own, kindled in him
    your eloquent fires. You talk, then sit,
and he gets up—it's the morning star introducing the sun
    whose blaze is bright, but the star still hangs in the sky
for those who know how and where to look. And for such as you
    to let it be known that you esteem the writings
of a poet who's out of favor, in exile . . . My heart goes out
    as it would to a gentle brother, for surely spirits
have their clans and kinships. One farmer knows
    and loves another farmer's steady patience;
a soldier loves and respects the bravery of a soldier;
    a sailor knows and admires the craft of the pilot.
You are a devotee of the Muses, as I am too.
    Talented you look kindly upon talent,

whether in prose or verse. It's the same fire the words
    will catch, their letters writhing to life in the heat.
We sit at the same desk, offering up our sweat
    on the same altar, and follow the same rites.
We share the professional's tough appraisal of work with words,
    reading what others write with a specially knowing
gimlet eye. I delight all the more to have your approval,
    a craftsman and judge of the craft. And I salute you
as one old campaigner come back to the Forum (I wish!)
    salutes another whose toils may have been remote
from Rome and those of his own but are yet familiar: Brother!
    May your friend and former pupil continue to show
his gratitude and affection and keep you in high regard.
    I pray that one day he may take control
of the world's reins to steer it with strong and steady hands,
    to which, the world's "Amen" is universal.

II, 6   TO GRAECINUS

In song Graecinus, Naso greets you, in an improvement—
    or is it a disimprovement?—from the plain
speech that used to serve us, face to face. I write,
    in any event, in an exile's faint and plaintive
voice here by the Pontus (where the choice is this or silence).
    I hear you condemn the embarrassing sins of your old
friend and suggest my sufferings aren't severe enough,
    considering what I deserve. And maybe you're right.
But doesn't it seem a bit late in the day for that?
    What's the point? Lighten up, old buddy!
I have, after all, confessed. It's over with; the time
    for your good advice was before the wreck occurred.

Now that my ship is sundered on black rocks, your warnings
    are useless, absurd. You can, if you choose, hold out
a hand to one in distress and support the chin of a drowning
    man who flails in the water—as you've been doing,
and as you would want others to do for you. I pray
    your mother, wife, brothers, and all your house
may be free from such ills as I have suffered, as you must pray
    with heart and voice for me. I hope you enjoy
Caesar's continued approval. Anything else would be foul:
    foul to turn away from a friend; foul
to abandon a ship in distress; foul to bend to the winds
    of fortune, disclaiming those who do not prosper.
In the storybooks we read when we were little children,
    how else could heroes behave? Did Orestes
and Pylades abandon each other? Not in my
    edition. Or Theseus and Pirithous?
The ages have admired their steadfastness and applauded—
    as they will, I have no doubt, admire you.
Praise is the just reward for loyalty, and my thanks
    will never be dumb. As long as these lines live,
as long as Latin lasts, your name will go down as a model
    of how a friend can behave. You are my steed.
I trust you with my life to bear me up—and forgive,
    the touch, from time to time, of a needful spur.

II, 7   TO ATTICUS

From the Getan badlands, my letter comes to you with good
    wishes, Atticus. How goes life for you?
And I wonder how it goes for me with you—do I keep
    a place, still, in your heart? I ought not doubt,

but I take nothing for granted and dread at every step
      the treacherous footing. I pray you will indulge me.
Even unruffled waters can scare a shipwreck survivor;
      a fish that has once felt the hook is wary
of the bronze barb that every morsel thereafter may hide;
      the lamb, afraid of the wolf, may even flee
the protecting sheepdog . . . Or better, think of a man with a
                                    wound
      who can't help but shrink from the doctor's touch.
It doesn't make any sense: one understands but can't
      help flinching. What's happened to me has changed me,
made me gun-shy, turned me jumpy, turned my mental
      landscape ghastly. Every random shadow
is quick with menace. The world has changed, turned
      inimical, inhospitable, the gods
are implacable. Even Fortune, no longer fickle, has steadied
      to hold me fast in her malign regard.
It sounds implausible? Yes, I agree, it does, for the long
      string of my woes and losses breaks all rules,
defies reason itself so that calculation is pointless,
      as it is in a field of wheat, each ear, each grain
a blur no eye can accommodate, no mind take in.
      Instead, by the blooms in a rolling meadow of thyme,
by the birds in a wheeling flock, the fish in a gleaming school,
      reckon my hurts of land and air and sea.
Nowhere in all the world is there a more savage and brutish
      tribe than the Getans, my neighbors, but even they
are pained to hear my misfortunes, a full accounting of which
      would run on, hypnotic, grand, my catalogue
of the ships, every one of them wrecked, foundered, sunk.
      If I fear to hear how you think of me these days,
it's nothing you've done or failed to do, but only me
      and my terrible luck. Whatever bad can happen,
will. And it looms. And I fear it. I cannot remember
      what carelessness was, or joy. Grief is my habit,

my keeper, the only mirror in which I can recognize
    my face, care-worn and scarred as a rock water
has pock-marked so that there's no space left for any new
    blow's bruise. I'm worn thin as an old
plowshare some poor peasant leaves to his eldest son.
    My heart is an Appian Way for the wagon wheels
and hoofs to pound with one burden after another.
    In the hope of renown, men devote their lives
to art; my gifts brought me only disgrace and ruin.
    My life was blameless—much good has that done me.
It's hardly a comfort to think of my unrewarded virtues.
    Serious sinners are pardoned—because their friends
have prayed for them; my friends are all of a sudden mutes.
    Some have managed to plead in their own behalf—
in order to manage that, you have to be there at the ear
    of power: I was away at the critical time
and could say nothing to help myself. The silent displeasure
    of Caesar is fearsome enough, but what he said
of me aloud, aroused, was everywhere reported.
    It was terrible, ill luck piled upon ill luck:
the dead of winter, storms, rough seas, and bitter cold;
    no friend in sight but only a ravening horde
eager to take advantage, to profit from my misfortunes;
    the worst possible venue, the most dismal,
the farthest from Rome, the least protected, the most barren . . .
    The abraded soul can sometimes find some solace
in tending a garden: I look out on a barren, stony
    field, its poor stalks stunted by icy
Sarmatian winds and broken by hostile raiders' horses'
    hoofs that have crossed and then swept back again.
The nervous, the near mad can take a kind of comfort
    in the gentle purling of streams and the play of light
on running water; here the rivers are dun and dull
    or brackish when the tide runs. Everything stinks

or is broken, or they are fresh out of it, or they never
    heard of it . . . All I'm going on here is nerve,
courage, more than I thought I had. I am not mad;
    I hang on; I do exercise; I keep
my chin up and my head comparatively high—
    to let go even a little is to fall
completely apart. It's stupid, and yet I continue to hope,
    imagining how one day the prince's ire
may yet melt. To give up on that would be to give up
    absolutely. You and a few friends
have held fast, as I hold fast to you, believing
    in your belief, without which I would drown.

II, 8   To Cotta Maximus

The Caesars have come—that medal you sent that shows
                                  Augustus,
    Tiberius, and Livia, in profile
gracing the silver as if it were gold. Or say that the ore
    was twice refined, for had I gotten ingots,
they couldn't have weighed as much as this icon of the faces
    of the gods to whom I pray for what cannot
be bought at any price. These are the only stars
    in my murky sky; theirs is the constellation
by which I steer. You have, with your gift, translated me back
    to Rome and brought me suddenly, safely home.
These are the faces I used to see on great occasions,
    and once more I salute them, as I hardly
dared hope ever again to do. If I were
    back home I could imagine no greater honor

than what you have contrived for me. What else do I need?
    A forum or two? Hills? Temples? All that
can be filled in, the imagination promptly supplying
    peripheral details. I gaze on Caesar
and see the Rome that he embodies, the real Rome.
    I stare at his face and try to read its mood.
Anger? Directed at me? I know it's merely a likeness,
    but a concentrated enough gaze can melt
metal, inspirit mere matter. I hope to produce
    a change of expression, a softening there of the eyes
and mouth, and pray aloud to the lord of the world to spare me
    for the sake of his own glory and that of Rome.
Restrain your just wrath, I pray—by the gods who are never
    deaf to prayer; by your consort, who is your only
equal; and by your son, like you a model of virtues.
    I stare at the three faces and think I see them
move in my hand. They quiver to life in the blur of my brimming
    tears, as I beg: Lighten my burden. Let
me be moved from here; grant me another home
    far from the Scythian crazies, noble Caesar!
And you, Tiberius, Caesar next to Caesar, kindly
    attend to my prayer and wish me well as I
have wished for your success with the German tribes as wild
    as ours here, that they may be cowed and tamed
to obey the crack of your whip or that of your crack troops.
    I offer a Health to your father, that he may attain
Nestor's age; and your mother that she may equal in years
    the Cumaean Sibyl; may you continue as son
for a long time. And you, Livia, I invoke,
    implore that you hear my prayers of you and for you—
that your husband live in safety, and your grandsons and their
    children. I pray that Drusus, whom the cruel
Germans took from you may be your family's only
    bereavement. I pray that his brother may avenge

that loss and, wearing the purple, drive the snow-white horses
　　of the triumph's car. O you kind gods, listen!
Hear my fawning prayers! See how I am reduced . . .
　　Let it be some advantage to me to have
your faces here before me. Into the Coliseum,
　　Caesar comes, and the gladiators are glad,
knowing his reputation for mercy and how their prospects
　　have suddenly brightened. I breathe that same sigh
of relief and rejoice to see that benevolent face, or better,
　　three benevolent faces here in my own
room. How happy are those who have the chance to encounter,
　　instead of these representations, the actual faces.
What fate, niggard and hostile, begrudges, art can supply,
　　and I should be churlish not to cherish its gift.
How else do we know those gods whom the icy ether hides?
　　In Jupiter's temple we worship an artist's likeness,
marble craft has turned holy. And I shall make it my care
　　to keep this medal enshrined. I'd rather lose
my head, would sooner allow my eyes to be gouged from their
　　　　　　　　　　　　　　　　　　　　　　　　　　sockets

　　than suffer the loss of this trebly precious icon.
Here in my exile, it shall protect me, comfort, inspire,
　　when the Getae besiege and threaten to overwhelm.
Am I crazy? Has too much yearning turned me silly—to hope
　　help is at hand, that my gods have heard? Their features
do seem less stern, their lips about to smile, their eyes
　　gentled. I pray my madness may be prophetic
and sane. It can happen, their wrath, however just,
　　waning as the wounds of the gods heal.

II, 9   TO KING COTYS

Progeny of kings, Cotys, whose line goes back
      even to Eumolpus, Neptune's son—
word may have reached your ears that I am here in your
      part of the world, in a land adjoining your own,
a suppliant, desperate. Hear, O gentle youth, my cry
      and give what aid you can to someone in need,
an exile. Fortune has dealt me a truly terrible hand
      in which you are the wild card, my one golden
ray of hope. A shipwrecked sailor, I staggered ashore;
      the natives could have been hostile, an even greater
menace than all those heaving mountains of water behind me.
      Instead, I find your friendly welcome and take
heart to see that my luck has bottomed out, improves . . .
      How noble a thing it is, how royal, to extend
a hand to raise the fallen. How can a generous nature
      better declare itself, enthroned or not?
Power is always awesome: what we admire is power
      put to good purpose, that does not permit
prayers of the weak to go unanswered. But you know this,
      have always understood what is in your blood,
the heritage of Eumolpus, founder of your line,
      and of Erichthonius too, Minerva's child
by Vulcan. The several gods and demigods, the heroes
      whose names bedeck your family tree have left you,
as part of your legacy, this—the desire to do what you can
      for beggars who pluck at your robe's hem and plead
for help. Why else would we pray to the gods or build shrines
      and temples to do them honor? The world is harsh,
and life is short and sad, but sometimes the gods hear,
      and intercede, when pity wells up like water
in mountain springs and their hearts melt to see how it is
      with us poor mortals. They can change things.

At least, they can offer hope. Why else sacrifice
     on Jupiter's altars? Or Neptune's? Who but sailors
and travelers come to his temples? The farmer praying to Ceres
     hopes for decent treatment, just as the vintner
who sacrifices a goat to Bacchus wants his vines
     and vats to produce. And so we pray to Caesar.
It's not a tradesman's bargain. Nobody keeps accounts
     down to the last dinar—but as between
gentlemen, decent people who mean to do one another
     well, there is a reservoir of good will
we create for one another and sometimes need to draw on.
     Among civilized men, the rules are clear
for the decencies that govern the host-guest connection—
     and I am, after all, a kind of guest.
In the name of your worthy father, I invoke that code and those
     rules of behavior. Who does not curse the awful
Antiphates, the Laestrygonian king who killed
     strangers and ate their flesh? Who does not bless
Alcinous, for his gracious welcome to that stranger
     who turned out to be Ulysses. And you
are no monster or tyrant. Fierce in time of war,
     you prefer to be gentle in peace. A man of learning,
a patron of arts and crafts, a connoisseur of refinement,
     you are, in the largest sense, a humane man.
A poet, too—and I have read and admired your work.
     Had your name been removed from the pages, I couldn't
                                             have guessed
their author came from Thrace. Orpheus isn't the only
     singer these parts can boast of. I salute you!
The arts of war and peace rarely combine together
     in one man, but when you take off your armor,
you pick up the pen to scale the Muses' difficult mountain—
     a tough climb to the starry Pierian heights,
as only those who have made the attempt can understand.
     That knowledge is something else we share, comrades,

163

or votives at least at the same shrine. I extend my arms
    in solemn prayer, bard to bard, brother
to brother, to ask for your protection. I come to your shores
    guilty of no crime. I am no killer,
counterfeiter, or fraud. I broke no laws except
    those of taste perhaps. To my *Art of Love,*
I plead guilty, and also to other errors of judgment
    on which we need not dwell. Whatever it was,
my punishment was carefully calibrated—Caesar
    relegated me, deprived me of Rome,
but nothing else. I am not a political problem. There's nothing
    in the least degree awkward here, I promise.
What I ask is well within your power—merely to keep me
    safe and secure, alive in a place I hate.

II, 10   To Macer

Guess who, Macer! Maybe you recognize the seal?
    Or if that isn't enough, you can open the letter
and examine the handwriting . . . Have you figured it out yet?
    Has it been so long, has all memory faded
of your old friend Naso? Yes, it's me! Has time,
    that cowardly sneak-thief, cleaned you out
so that on the shelves and vitrines of your memory's salon, your

                                                 old

    mementoes and association items
are gone? (Or were they just too much trouble to dust?)
    I can't believe it! Too many years, too many
good times for that to have happened. And through my wife,
    we are, after all, related. But more important,

we're both poets. We were, and still remain, colleagues—
    albeit that your talent was never frittered
pointlessly away on a naughty *Art*. You were
    a serious fellow, and shrewder than I ever was.
My lessons in louche living came back to haunt me, the gay
    dog hounded out of town (poetic
justice, I guess). We went our separate ways, but the rites
    we followed were much the same: the baleful blank
page we faced each morning, and the same fears to conquer . . .
    I think of you at your desk, as you must think
of me and wish to lighten the burden of my misfortunes.
    Surely you recall those trips we took!
You were the one who first showed me the cities of Asia.
    You took me down to Sicily, to the temples,
to Aetna's spectacular show as Typhon's gargle of flame
    lit the night sky. Together we saw the crystal
spring of Arethusa, and Palicus' sulphurous pools.
    That trip we took took up most of a year,
and I think about it here, in a Getan land of unlikeness
    where nothing at all is lovely, splendid, or holy.
I remember how you made the arduous trip a pleasure,
    whether aboard ship or on some bumpy
and rutted road—you smoothed the way with jokes and stories.
    There were more words than steps. The summer days
were never long enough and the sun would go down and the sky
    redden and fade to black, and we would be
babbling on like morning birds. We were *Wanderjahr*
    companions: we risked the road's perils, the sea's
dangers, and even each other's derision as we revealed
    our highest aspirations, our deepest dreams,
our darkest fears, as young men do. We could, without
    thinking, speak our hearts, uncircumspect,
direct. Think of those days, for when you do, I am
    there before you. And as I think of you here,

under the heavens' icy pivot, you are with me,
    beside me again, the ideal person to talk to.
But it's better that you should think of me and thereby bring me
    out of this terrible place and back to the comforts
I miss of the wonderful city, familiar sights and old
    friends . . . I am at home in your good heart.

II, 11   TO RUFUS

This comes to you scribbled in haste and, I fear, crudely,
    from Naso, an artless effusion of the author
of the ill-starred *Art,* from a whole world's width away,
    where I keep you nevertheless close in mind—
on the short list of those who have kept the faith of friendship.
    I'd sooner gasp my life's last breath away
on the empty air than forget how you've stood by me and what
    I owe you for tears that streamed down your cheeks
when my own eyes, in shock, unblinking were stone dry.
    My wife, whom I cannot ever praise enough,
has had occasion to thank you for words of consolation
    and admonition. In the exercise of virtue,
even the most adept athletes can use a coach.
    You have been to her the uncle that Castor
was to Menelaus' daughter; you've been as Hector
    was to his nephew, Iulus, a model, a guide,
understanding how much the human spirit is able
    to bear a burden of grief. She follows your
example, takes instruction from you, and proves herself
    with your approval. What she would have done
and borne without urging, she manages all the better
    with your help, as the high-spirited horse

will race the faster having a clever jockey up.
    May the gods reward you as I have not the power
myself to do! What I can only imagine, they
    see clearly and cannot but recognize.
Faith should have its reward: I pray they send you health,
    that you thrive for years in Latium's golden sun.

Book III

III, 1   To His Wife

I stare out at a leaden sea that Jason's oars
    so long ago whipped silver, and I turn
to barren land behind me, as flat as if it cowered
    from assaults of storms, and storms of assaulting raiders.
When will I ever escape this nightmarish landscape, when
    will I shake from the soles of my shoes its bitter dust?
By your leave, I'd take my leave—not walk or run, but dance
    away, assuming only my spirit has managed
to last till then, that I haven't been planted in some shallow
    hole in the gray clay that now confronts me,
my Tomis tomb. By your gracious leave, I tell you frankly
    that nothing of my exile is harder to bear
than that it's here, that it looks like this, that every morning
    this sky, sea, and landscape blight the day,
and turn my sadness bitter, spiteful and unrelenting.
    There's never a gentle moment in early spring
when the buds burst forth, nor a golden autumn harvest.
    Nature has no remedy here but cold,
always a damp cold that makes the bones and joints
    ache. There is ice on the river, and out in the harbor
the fish swim with a roof of ice over the black
    water. We have no trees but only stunted
sickly things no taller than bushes, so that the land
    is bare as the sea, browner, but otherwise
the same waste space. Springs here bubble forth
    with sulfurous water that leaves you thirsty as ever.
And the birds don't sing but only croak like frogs or chirr
    like the bugs that swarm in wormwood—the only crop
of this accursed place. We live, meanwhile, in fear
    of savages, marauders with poisoned tips
on their spears and arrowheads. Our blood, already cold,
    chills further to hear their wild warwhoops.

By land it's hard to get here; it's also risky by sea;
      and to live here, moment by perilous moment, is torture
you can't ever get used to. You cannot simply learn
      to survive this way—which is why, after all these years,
I still beg to be moved to some place less bizarre.
      To wish is not enough; to want and weep
and pray is not enough; we have to do, to strive,
      persistently active, passionate day and night,
tireless, shameless, using our friends and their friends too.
      I know it's asking a lot, but I'm not asking
anything: it's the situation, the weird way Caesar
      has made me even more famous than I was
or dreamt of being, or wanted to be. And now the poems
      are famous and you are famous, whether or not
you or I would have chosen any such thing. Your name
      is made or unmade here, by what you do
or fail to do to meet the challenge fate has thrown us.
      Fame will judge the three of us, you and me
and Caesar too—as Capaneus became famous
      when the lightning bolt of Zeus transformed his whole
existence into a single electrifying moment,
      and when Amphiarius' horses diappeared
into the earth's maw, he too felt Fame's rough
      hug, squeezing everything else away,
all he'd ever been or done. Catastrophes do that:
      Ulysses' long voyage; Philoctetes'
wound; and now, in my humbler way, Naso's exile.
      It catapults us upwards where we join
the constellations' dizzy dance where we shall whirl
      together forever. I'm sorry for many things,
bitterly sorry for many burdens I've laid upon you.
      This is the heaviest yet, and with this one also,
I couldn't help it. My praises will ring either true or false,
      sincere or ironic, according to how it's perceived

that you behaved. I've put a spotlight on you, and now
    the world will decide whether your life has been
caring and active enough. Or will you be called indifferent
    to the plight of your wretched husband away in exile?
A sick thought, I admit. But I am sick now, fevered.
    My pulse is erratic. My doctor shakes his head
and tries to look sympathetic—it's all he knows how to do.
    I turn in my last extremity, hold out my hand
and ask you to do for me what I would do for myself
    if only I had the strength. But you are strong,
and we love each other. Married, we owe a debt to each other!
    Your own virtue compels you to help the helpless.
It's a family obligation all you Fabians boast of—
    and properly so. I once was a loving husband,
a not altogether worthless escort. I made you laugh.
    And wasn't it sometimes entertaining to be
the poet's wife? For such trivial services I
    demand a rate of return that is nothing less
than usury. But it's need rather than greed that drives me.
    Go from house to house, if you must, to plead
my case in every ear, let them all know I suffer,
    and beg them for your sake as well as my own
to let me be moved to a less bleak and dreadful region.
    I know I'm asking an awful lot, but should you
not succeed, you run no danger, nor will you risk
    any discomforts. You do not require these
promptings of mine? I know. But the world must also know.
    And it can't hurt, can it, for me to encourage
what your own spirit urges—just as the brave are braver
    when the notes of the battle trumpet sound in their ears.
You can take this as your warrant, or even as your excuse
    for being a pest (as I trust you sometimes are).
No one can blame you for what you do in my behalf,
    taking up the Amazons' battle-axe

and brandishing in your other hand their crescent-shield.
 Implore the numinous Caesar not to be friendly
but only a little less hostile than heretofore. Your tears
 must move his spirit. And you and I can rely
on the welling up of tears, a freshet, a waterspout.
 If tears were coins, you and I would be richer
than anybody in Rome. Any my gratitude is as great
 as that of Admetus was for his wife, Alcestis.
Your legend will stand with hers, and Penelope's, or better
 with that of Laodamia, noble wife
of Protesilaus the first Achaean to fall at Troy—
 to be his companion in death, she killed herself,
as did Euadne, who threw herself on her husband's pyre.
 But let's not be any gloomier than we have to.
It's better for me that you're alive and able to talk
 to Caesar's wife, two paragons together.
She is like Venus and Juno combined into one perfection,
 but do not fear to approach her. She is no
Medea, or Procne, or Clytemnestra, or Scylla, or Circe.
 She's no Medusa with snakes coiled on her head,
but the foremost of women: she proves that the Fates sometimes
 can pick the right people on whom to lavish
earthly rewards, for she, next only to Caesar,
 is the one on whom the sun's rays glint the brightest,
a diamond. Choose your time well, as a cautious sailor
 consults the sky before putting out to sea.
Even the oracles sometimes fall silent, and gates at the shrines
 of the greatest gods are on occasion shut.
Look to the city's mood and the empire's peace, that no
 frown may cloud the brows of Augustus' household
(I pray that is ever the case) and at the auspicious and right
 moment, approach, expectant, confident, steady . . .
You must not seem to hurry. If they are busy, come back
 at another time. You can always try again.

But neither must you defer too long or wait for a perfect
 moment when she is absolutely idle,
for that will never present itself. Rely on your instincts!
 Don't defend me—don't go down that road—
but weep, sink down, and lying there on the floor stretch forth
 your arms toward her immortal feet to plead
that I may be taken away from a battle zone. Say only
 that Fortune itself is all the foe I can handle.
There's more I've thought of, but never mind. I shouldn't tax you
 beyond your endurance. I hear you stammering out
the first couple of lines, you've rehearsed and learned by heart . . .
 And then you have to break off—and she perceives
your dread of her majesty, feels your leaden grief, and sees
 your tears and hears your sobs, more eloquent far
than anything I could plan for you in advance to try
 to convey. Reason will yield as it always does
to emotion. Show your feelings, therefore, and she will feel
 with and for you. It isn't manipulation
or any kind of feigning but the simplest truth of your grief
 and love for me that will be in the end persuasive.
Trust yourself, as I trust you with all my heart
 and soul! But pick a lucky day and hour
for heaven's sake. And go to a temple first to kindle
 a fire upon some holy altar and offer
incense and wine to the gods whose help we both implore.
 Ask for the gods' help, which is all we have
left to hope for. Any of them may hear your prayers,
 but of all the gods, the deity of Augustus
is the one to whom you must direct yourself, to him,
 his offspring, and his consort. May they hear
the words you speak; may they see your tears; and may they feel
 what you and I feel—and answer our prayer.

III, 2   TO COTTA

Dear—and you truly are—Cotta: I send you sincere
    wishes for your good health in the salutation
with which it's the custom to open a letter. For me to know
    you are well is a real comfort, reducing a little
my anguish out here. The storm was terrible—many abandoned
    ship; others were washed away by the waves
that broke over my prow. But you, my friend, held fast,
    a last anchor to keep my shattered vessel
from swamping and going down. I can never thank you enough
    for the loyalty and courage you have displayed.
The others, I pardon—human nature is not what I'd thought.
    I've learned a bitter lesson—but part of that teaches
how to appreciate someone like you. I understand,
    better than you do, yourself, how rare you are!
The timbers in some public building creak and the warning
    not only scatters the crowd but turns them into
absurd creatures who scurry, antlike. That's how they ran,
    crazy with panic, reduced, no longer men
but something less. It's easy to write them off. They're another
    species, really. Whatever it is they think,
it doesn't affect their behavior; they merely react, instinctive
    and out of control. One can't argue with that,
blame it, or worry about it. For some I make excuses . . .
    But what does it matter? I don't get invitations
to dinner out here from any of them. Or send them either.
    Let them know by this that I forgive them,
whatever that's worth. But for you, the very few, the precious
    handful who couldn't imagine behaving that way,
who just didn't understand what it was to be terrified,
    for you people, my debt of thanks is such
that I trust my gratitude may outlive my flesh. My ashes
    long cold and scattered, yet will my words

resound through the decades with your richly deserved praises.
    Your grandchildren's grandchildren will show
these verses to their own children, proud that they bear
    the name of someone like you. Even out here,
at the back door of the empire, the Sauromatian hordes
    and Getan rabble know who you are. Your fame
is legendary among the barbarian herdsmen and raiders—
    for I have learned a bit of the local dialects,
have a few phrases of Getic, and can make myself understood
    in Sarmatian. And I've told them of you, my friend,
steadfast, loyal, and true. One of the local sages
    nodded his head, pulled at his long beard,
and answered me, saying: "We know what friendship is.
    Our country and yours are as distant as any;
but we are not all that different. In Scythian Tauri, I
    was born and raised. It's hard country, and proud
we are to be its sons! Our people worship the goddess
    of Phoebus' pallid comapnion, in her splendid
temple where once her image stood, and the pedestal yet
    remains. The altar stones that used to be white
are dark from the blood that the virgin priestesses poured

                                  upon them,
    sacrificing strangers. The rite is cruel
but old. It goes back to the earliest times of our people, when
                                    Thoas
    ruled that part of the world. He held the scepter
and very nearly dropped it when Iphigenia came
    blown on the wind, flying through thin air—
although painters give her a little pufflet of cloud to crouch on.
    She alighted here and assumed the priestess' role
for years performing Hecate's gory rites, until
    that sailing ship appeared with the two young men,
strangers to our shores: Orestes, her brother,
    and Pylades, his friend. Fame keeps their names

bright and bound together, as they were bound and dragged
    to the altar, sprinkled with lustral water, blessed,
and the ceremonial veils were draped over their heads.
    You know the story—how she apologized
for the cruel rite, and asked what land these two had come from
    in their ill-fated ship. And when they told her
they came from her own city, her heart pounded with pity
    and she offered to spare one of them, to let
one go home as messenger, bearing the terrible tidings.
    And Pylades chose death and bade his friend
go, and take what she offered. But Orestes also chose
    death for himself and urged his friend to flee.
They argued back and forth, agreed that the plan was sound,
    but differed on the one detail of which
should be the one to die. Meanwhile she prepared
    her letter for whichever to take back home—
to Orestes, her brother, to come and save his suffering sister . . .
    The priests and the sages spin it out, but the end
is always the same and always deeply satisfying.
    There is that wonderful moment when light breaks
upon them, that he, himself, is Orestes, the brother to whom
    she is making her appeal. They grab the precious
statue of Diana and flee in the night, back
    to the ship and over the trackless waters, the currents,
the winds right and steady, as love between two friends
    deserves. And from that time even to this,
through all the years that have passed, their names persist in that
                                        air

    that carried Iphigenia here." The sage
fell silent then, and the others took up the subject with stories
    of acts of devotion, for even on this wild
and bleak shore, or perhaps especially here in the teeth
    of savage nature, friendship is what men value
and trust, because they are forced to rely on one another.
    Back in Rome one takes them rather for granted,

but here such deeds as yours can move the hearts of stern
    and hardened men. They may not understand
high birth or gentle manners; they wouldn't know a single
    one of the famous forebears on your family
tree, but that you stood by a friend in disgrace and need
    they can understand well enough and have, from me,
learned how to praise. Were you to make the arduous journey
    you would be welcomed here as "the famous Cotta,"
whose worth is such as one finds in those who begin a line
    as distinguished as yours. And they are by no means wrong,
for your ancestors, as famous as all of them are, would be proud
    of how you've maintained and even improved their name.

III, 3   To Maximus

If you have a few spare minutes, a blank space on the page
    of your daybook, Maximus, maybe you'll give me a quarter
hour to listen. I'll tell you what happened, or what I think
    I didn't dream. It was nighttime, but bright outside
with a full moon pouring its syrupy light through my bedroom
                                window.
    I was asleep, but I heard a peculiar noise,
a whirring of wings and the creaky sound of a shutter moving.
    Startled, I sat up, rubbed my eyes into focus,
and looked—to find Amor, the god of Love, standing
    at the foot of my bed, his hand on its maple post.
He was never an old buddy, but I'd known him to say hello to,
    and he looked awful, his hair a mess, his feathers
drooping down. And those pretty baubles he used to wear
    were all gone, those necklaces, rings, and gewgaws

nowhere in sight. I blinked, cleared my throat, and asked him
    "What in hell are you doing here? You've come
to see how bad it is where I am, here at the Danube's
    drain? Haven't you done me enough harm
already? This is your fault," I told him, waving an arm
    to the bleak prospect outside the window through which
he'd come. "You were the one who first suggested the poems
    that caused all the fuss! It was your terrific
idea to set those naughty tricks you so much enjoyed
    hearing about into couplets. You are the one
who ought to be living here, while I should be back in Rome
    turning out tragedies, epics, the work I always
supposed was the proper task of a serious poet. But no,
    you and your wicked mother have absolutely
ruined my life. What more do you want now? To gloat?
    Be my goddamn guest! I hope you're proud
of what you've done. My talent may not have been so amazing,
    but it served to accomplish what you had in mind for me
to do. Did you like watching while I mutilated myself,
    cutting my own throat with my pen? Look out
that window and see where it's got me, all that clever, risqué
    stuff I scribbled. It was your fault, you hoodlum!"
I waited for him to answer but he didn't. He wouldn't open
    his mouth. He simply stood there down at the end
of the bed making that little moue he thinks is cute.
    "Never mind," I told him, "that you are immortal
while I am not, there are still a couple of minimal rules,
    decencies gods and men have both agreed to observe.
And one of those is that pupils should show a certain respect
    to teachers and masters. Think of how King Numa
treated Pythagoras. Think of the Phrygian Satyr who taught
    Olympus to play the flute, or Eumolpus, whom Orpheus
                                                        gave

the cult secrets. I could go on, but you get my drift—
    from time's beginning, I am the only teacher

abused this way, whose own student has so betrayed him.
        You could have come forward at least to say
what you knew perfectly well was true—that I never corrupted
        a single innocent girl or respectable bride
or matron, but wrote only for those who already were fooling
        around on the wrong side of the sheets. You can
tell them! You were there and remember how I wrote
        those silly things and for whom! You are my witness!
And after I published the poems, you—who hang out in the

                                                    seamier

        parts of town—can attest that the main response
of the blades and bloods was nothing but moderate laughter!
        You have the power, the prestige, not to mention
those arrows that pierce armor; you have that flaming torch
        that lights your way through the darkness; you also enjoy
a blood connection to Caesar, whose ancestor, Aeneas,
        was your own brother. By all that, I implore you,
persuade Caesar, make him forget his anger against me,
        let him at least assent to the modest humane
suggestions my friends have made that I might be translated
        to somewhere a little less bleak and forbidding than this
cold and benighted place." That's what I said to the lad,
        the imp-god, who nodded his head in agreement.
"What you're saying," he answered, "is perfectly true. I never
        learned anything wicked from you, no crime,
no bad tricks from your *Art*—I could swear by my arrows, my

                                                    mother,

        by whatever you like. But what good would that do?
You know as well as I do, it wasn't only the poem
        that got you sent out here, but the other business
—we needn't go into details—which is out my jurisdiction.
        And I agree with Caesar that, "crime" or "error,"
whatever you want to call it, you got what you deserved,
        you poor sap—which is why I am here and why

I've traveled this far, to try to cheer you a little, to pay
    a call as one might on a friend who has been unwell."
Pleased with himself, he made a stagey bow and told me,
    "I've been here before, you know. It was long ago
when Mother sent me to strike Medea's heart. This time
    I come for a gentler purpose, to gladden yours
with my guess that Caesar's may soften, and your prayers may be
                       answered
    at long last. The mood in Rome is euphoric;
Tiberius' triumph bathes the imperial house in a golden
    light of joy. They are all basking, rejoicing,
Livia, Caesar himself, and all the children. The people
    congratulate him and themselves, and every altar
flickers with fragrant flames. In the holy temples, prayers
    arise and will be heard—even yours, old sport!"
He winked, blew me a kiss, and either he floated away
    or I came back to my senses or else woke up.
An odd business, and yet I was sure you'd want to hear
    what's going on—as sure as I am that swans
and milk and polished ivory aren't black. Your birth
    and your spirit are matched in nobility, Maximus. Candor
and honor are what you inherit from Hercules, your forebear.
    You don't even know what envy is or meanness
that creeps like a snake on the ground, for you spirit soars aloft.
    I send you my dream and prayer—a lesser man
might see in it only bibliographical value, but you
    will know what it is, a suppliant's plea, and treat it
and me with the generous spirit you've always shown the poor
    and despised, among which group you must now count me.

III, 4   To Rufinus

These words, Rufinus, come from Tomis, civilization's
    last outpost's suburb, where even Rome's
might gives way to barbarism and empty space.
    The Salute I send is more than a formal greeting.
However unprepossessing it seems, still it has traveled
    a long way to join in the great parade,
as the spectators understand. They look at the curious costumes,
    notice the odd instruments, and adjust
their standards—as I now beg you to do for me and my work.
    A better piece wouldn't need such special favors
as I ask for here. But years of hardships and bitter
    sorrows have dulled my talents. Whatever sheen
they once had is gone—if it ever was there. I wonder
    if I wasn't kidding myself, if friends and readers
were being kind or polite. I rely on your generous nature
    to maintain that old fiction, for if that's gone,
I've nothing left. I labor under a great disadvatage;
    other writers have seen Tiberius' triumph,
and when they describe it, they have the gods at their sides, as

                                    helpers
    and research assistants. They transcibe the events
just as they happened, while I must rely on rumors, hearsay,
    what I remember, and what my imagination
can conjure up as detail, grist for my passion's mill.
    The silver and gold are easy; the gorgeous colors
I can assume; but the faces, the look in the eyes of the captive
    soldiers and chieftains, those would have been a help.
And the crowd's excitement, surely, the way men's hearts can move
    together like fish in a shoal, that thrilling sense
of being a part of a great occasion would have ignited
    even the dullest talent to make it bright.

A raw recruit, they say, can catch the regiment's spirit
 and his heart will beat to their drum and partake of their
 courage.
Mine is cold as the ice that has stopped the Danube's mouth,
 as dead as this dreary landscape, but even I
should have been revived, inspired, could have felt the warmth,
 the fervor

 stirring again. But one must make do somehow.
I don't even know the chieftain's names or the names of the towns
 the signs proclaimed. I have to rely on you
to make allowance. Supply what I lack—details, the fire,
 grace, elegance, everything. Even the mood
of rejoicing is hard for me now. My lyre is shabby, cracked,
 and doesn't do well anymore in the major keys.
Triumph is rather a reach. I barely remember the words
 in which to exult—I'm like a man in the dark
who stumbles into the sun and the brightness dazzles him blind;
 spots of the old blackness dance on his eyeballs.
You also have to allow for my tardiness. Homage is best
 when it's fresh and timely, and anyone with a pen
has taken his shot already. The readers' thirst is slaked,
 sated even, when I come by with my tray
of tepid drinks that nobody's grabbing. It's not my fault!
 Look where I'm living, how long it takes for news
to get here. I grab my pad and scribble as fast as I can
 to catch the next departure, but then there's a year or more
before that leaky tub makes it home again with my cargo
 of verses. Imagine a street vendor, his cart
full of those banners, badges, balloons, and souvenir tee-shirts,
 but who shows up at his corner six months late . . .
It's comedy, right? Or disaster! My colleagues back home, you
 other

 poets, are lucky. I mean you no disrespect,

but it's only fair to point out my handicap and to plead
    for any break I can get. Assume my work
comes from one who is dead, or the next worst thing to that,
    for the dead get a certain margin, a little leeway,
if only because they're beyond the reaches of malice and envy,
    as I ought to be, God knows. This life I lead
is a kind of death, as bleak and empty as anything Homer
    describes in those terrible scenes of his. I lack
earth piled up on my body, but there have been times when the
                                    wind
    howled and rolled the dust, so I thought to make good
on that one omission. Look, the proof is here in your hand:
    this woeful performance, well-intended but crude,
patched and splotched as it is, the work of a wraith's shadow,
    shows what I am and how I have been reduced.
All I can offer is weakness, pathos, and good intentions—
    and the fond idea that a poor but virtuous man,
approaching the altar, may hope his prayer may be heard and his
                                    lamb
    find favor as much as if he had offered an ox.
Were I at my best and brashest, this still would have been a project
    all but beyond me. A Vergil's stately power,
I never had. And these cock-eyed couplets I've made my habit
    are frail for such a burden—but what other meter
am I going to learn? The aged canine's range of performance
    doesn't enlarge, the adage says, but subtracts.
The hoop seems higher and smaller every year, and the poor
    beast takes longer to ready himself to jump.
I worry now, and I worry more that the next triumph
    I know is coming will find me even less
well prepared to sing paeans. The leaves are already in bud
    for the wreath they will place upon Caesar's noble head.
It's not just Ovid who says so, but the voice of the god speaking
    through me, or playing upon me like a whistle

he finds amusing because its sound is funny and shrill.
    Even from here at the Danube's bank, where wild
Getans lap the water like dogs, the word can come
    reliably of the future and what it holds.
Let Livia order the cars, the decorations, and set
    the order of march for the triumph. The Germans will drop
their spears and their hostile ways and Tiberius take up his pen
    to write the dispatch for messengers' horses to bring
quickly, quickly. And then, at more stately gaits, the other
    horses will come, caparisoned all in purple
and gold, bearing the hero home, his chaplets, his shield,
    his gold and bejewelled greaves glittering bright
in Roman sunshine. I see the trophies swaying and jouncing
    on tall poles and, behind them, captives in chains.
I see the floats of the vanquished towns, their broken walls
    with rivers around them flowing with spilled blood,
lifelike—deathlike—red. It will all happen, I know,
    and whatever my metric faults and stylistic lapses,
whatever my infelicities, this clear and accurate vision,
    this vatic gift I have must count for something.
I pray the gods may justify my uneven lines
    and demonstrate my heart's truth and my words'.

III, 5   To Maximus Cotta

You look at the blurry postmark and try to puzzle it out.
    Where has this limp missive limped in from?
Ah, where the Danube drains into the Pontus! Which also
    answers the next question—from whom it comes.
Whom else could you possibly know out here except poor Naso?
    He'd rather be meeting you vis-à-vis but sends

Greetings from Getan-world (and I wish I weren't
        here!). I also send congratulations,
having read the speech you gave and many times reread
        your excellent words, short and straight to the point.
But I have, by my repetitions, stretched out my pleasure in them.
        You do yourself—and your family, too—proud;
its long tradition of eloquence lives and prospers in you.
        On third and fourth inspections, the novelty fades,
but the strength of your argument's logic shows itself all the
                                                        clearer.
        It would have been good to have been there—water that's
                                                        brought
is sweet but never so fine as right from the spring, cold
        to chill your teeth! Or fruit arranged in a bowl
or heaped on a chased salver can never begin to compare
        with what you take from the tree, bending the bough
yourself to reach that perfection way out there at the tip.
        If I hadn't made a mess of my life, if my
Muse hadn't betrayed me, I should have heard your speech
        as one of the Centumvir Court judges, keeping
my face impassive, impartial, but deep within I'd have smiled
        at your elegant turns of phrase and my colleagues' nods
of approval. But there we are, or here I am—where Fate
        has dumped me, far from Rome and far from you.
Around me savages grunt in menace (which is a kind
        of unkind meaning), while I read Roman speeches!
They keep me alive! Continue to send me the proof
        (and the proofs in the long galleys) of your great talent.
And think of me sometimes, as I think of you so often.
        If you remember your friend, I am not quite dead,
as I hope this letter makes clear. So keep those cards and letters
        coming, my friend! They're food for a starving spirit!
I can hardly say what joy I take from the work of a young
        companion, in which I see the good results

184

of your studies of years ago—and therefore like to imagine
    that you sometimes think of me. You still write poems,
still read them to your friends or hand them the text and stand
    neither too close nor too far away, waiting
to hear what they think. You must in those edgy moments
                                        remember
    the old days, and your old friend, Naso, and miss him
at least a little . . . Out here, I live as much as I can
    in the past, and therefore, think of you all the time.
May Getic arrows impale me if I do not speak the truth—
    and those are as common out here as milkweed pods
that float on the air. It's terrible here, but the human heart
    has its own furlough program and goes where it will.
In that way I can return home, stalk through the city,
    visit, unseen, old haunts, greet my friends . . .
Look up! I'm probably there behind you, off to the left,
    beaming smiles and happy again. Believe it,
as we all try to believe in some kind of heaven. It helps
    to bear what we must wherever we are, to imagine
a better place. But here at the gate of hell, we live
    by such fancies. Don't say they're untrue.

III, 6   TO A FRIEND

From the Black Sea Riviera, Naso sends his greetings
    to an old friend . . . whose name he almost wrote.
But suppose I had. Suppose the pen had slipped, as the tongue
    so easily can, and I'd gone and blurted it out,
although you've asked me not to. What would happen? Others
    to whom I write have shown that there's no danger.

Caesar's a fair-minded man, as he he's demonstrated
    in my own case. Were I in his shoes and toga,
judging the deeds and misdeeds of somebody just like me,
    I'd do, in justice, just what he did. For years
I have been sending these letters back home to Rome, and no one
    I've named has suffered or had to apologize.
Caesar doesn't object to friendship. Letters of comfort
    to someone who suffers are hardly a federal case,
or even a misdemeanor. What can you possibly fear?
    And doesn't your worry, being groundless, display
distrust of the August gods? I'd imagine so, but my
    views are not much consulted these days on questions
of proper behavior. Still, it's the fact that a bolt of lightning
    can strike, and the victim survive, recover, go on
living . . . And then should his friends shun him as one whom
                           the god
    picked out to punish? Think of how Leucothea,
the sea nymph, came to Ulysses' aid, after Neptune wrecked
    his vessel. Swimming, choking, and trying not to
swallow salt water, he flailed—and did she avoid him, deny
    the help he needed? Of course not! The gods can show
mercy, can pity the desperate and wretched. There is no rule
    that tells them to hate the oppressed—and most of the gods
are less kindly than Caesar, who worships Justice and built her
    a temple some years ago, but all his life
has reverenced her at the shrine he keeps for her in his heart.
    The victims of Jupiter's thunderbolts are chosen
haphazardly—the villains and saints mixed in together;
    in Neptune's catch may be sinners, but he does throw
a wide net, and the innocent also gasp and die.
    In the lists of Mars, the rolls include the bravest
as he penalizes the virtue he ought to reward. What's fair
    or sane in that? Yet take a poll of us
whom Caesar has been driven to punish, and each and every
    man will say the same, confessing his fault,

and admitting the justice of what he is made to suffer. Suppose
    a mistake, however. They happen. But then the gods
cannot restore to life one whom their fire or water
    has taken, or battle destroyed; there is no appeal,
no possible commutation or pardon—as we whom Caesar
    punishes always hope for (and hope's glow
keeps us alive). There's no reason to fear that the giving
    of comfort to exiles is dangerous. Caesar is no
wicked Busiris or crazy Phalaris eager for victims'
    screams. Why should you fear the reefs in a calm
and placid sea? It's nonsense! And it makes me look bad too—
    as if I were the one who didn't trust our prince
to be fair and sane! But enough lecture. We'll look to the future,
    to other poems in which your name may yet
appear. It would shame us both if our friendship were never
                           mentioned!
    On the other hand, as a friend, I may not impose,
cannot dismiss your fears, however absurd they be.
    Except by your leave, I cannot pay you tribute,
for, open or secret, the friendship is more important than poems;
    one can't sit at a desk and create a friend.

III, 7   TO FRIENDS

Words fail me; they shrink from having to go through the same
    wheedle time after time. I am ashamed
of these prayers, as vain as they're endless, as you must be weary
    of being nagged. You know it now by heart,
don't even need to open the seal, but can guess the message.
    I shouldn't wonder if some smart kid isn't doing

an after-dinner impression of Ovid in Exile—as good
　　or as bad as what I do myself. But enough!
This will be different, I promise. I beg your several pardons,
　　admit and regret the error of all my hopes.
I'll stop my whining and begging, and won't even trouble further
　　my wife, that fine and virtuous woman who never
chose a career as a lobbyist—I can live with that.
　　I've borne worse. The bullock, cut from the herd,
detests the plow-yoke, bucks, and twists his muscular neck,
　　but after a while he learns, as I have learned
to endure what can't be helped. I'm here on the Getic shore,
　　and this is where I'm likely to end my days.
I'll expect that I shall be buried here where I've buried my hopes.
　　Hope is an odd companion; even a vain
and impossible dream can keep you going, but sooner or later
　　you wise up and you give it up for good,
if only because despair is so much less painful. The one
　　hope you retain is of death and its primitive mercy.
There are sailors who never learn to swim because they prefer
　　a quick end to the long, exhausting crawl
and the same salty swallow, but with arms heavy and hope
　　singing its mad song. Under these skies
I'm trapped as under a rock and I can't writhe free or crawl
　　away. There's no sense kidding myself or dreaming
of mercies from home. The struggle only increases the hurt.
　　Descriptions of Rome, descriptions of what I see
in my exile out here—they're both written in blood. Give up!
　　I swear I have! It's better this way than to keep
pestering friends to pester Caesar and always in vain!
　　The one petition worth trying can't come from you—
that I be allowed to die, that some minor clerk instruct
　　the commander here to deal with the problem and end it.
A guard could appear one night with the vial in his hand and a
　　　　　　　　　　　　　　　　　　　　　　　　sword
　　in case of need, but I shall be eager to drink.

III, 8   To Maximus

It's hardly a simple thing out here to select a gift
     to send back home as a token of our old friendship.
One thinks of silver or gold, but that's absurd in Tomis,
     where there aren't craftsmen's workshops or even mines.
The savages barely allow our farmers to scratch the earth's
     belly, much less let miners dig deep shafts.
Clothing perhaps? But the dyes out here are dreadful and weavers
     as crude as the wool of the scrawny and half-wild sheep.
Something to eat or drink, then, some delicate local tid-bit?
     Again, absurd! There's nothing here, no vines,
no orchards with rows of trees, their branches laden with fruit.
     It's coarse bread here and barely potable water,
and wormwood, which is all that this blasted heath is good for,
     the bitter yield of a bitter land . . . No, thank you!
In the whole region is nothing precious, sweet, or clever;
     the choices, then, are reduced to violence and pain,
our real wealth and our only export products. I send you
     a quiver full of Scythian arrows. Use them
in good health, or, as they say out here, "May they drink
     your enemies' blood!" You can hang them up on your wall
and tell your friends they are pens from Tomis, where writing is
                             always
     a matter of life and death, for such is our local
Muse. The joke is poor, I fear, but I am its butt:
     I pray you take it well, with a friend's grin.

III, 9   To Brutus

Because these lines of mine tend toward the same point always,
    you tell me there's criticism—I'm dreary and boring,
always whining, complaining, and begging that I might be moved
    to somewhere less outlandish . . . It's all true.
I haven't gone blind or lost my mind. I know what I'm doing,
    how well or badly. Writers tend to be fond
of their own productions as parents are of their children.
    Talk to any murderer's mother; you'll get
the predictable line about how "he was always a good boy."
    And Agrius said, when they asked what his ugly son
had been like as a child, "Thersites? A good-looking kid.
                                            Handsome!"
    I'm not so blind as that, can see the defects
in what I beget at this crude excuse for a writing table.
    Why don't I fix the flaws? Why do I let
the work go out this way, blemished, with boring stretches?
    To be able to diagnose is not quite the same
as to know how to cure. I look at a line sometimes, or a word,
    know that it's wrong, but don't have the strength or spirit
to fool with it any longer. I look out the window and see
    through my transparent reflection a grotesque landscape,
and I realize the whole undertaking is simply absurd. I'm
                                            undone—
    my belief in myself is undone—and nothing matters.
One word's as good as another. And any is better than none.
    The writing helps to pass the time; I escape,
or at least my spirit does, for an hour or two. But to fix
    is beyond my faith and endurance. An Aristarchus
can analyze but it takes a Homer to get it right.
    It also takes composure, steady attention,
and pride in one's work and self. That's what's eroded, gone
    for years. I look at that face in the window, distorted

and crazy, as I am crazy, as writing these lines is crazy . . .
 And what the hell difference does any one word make?
You think the Getans care? One grunt resembles another!
 Besides, when it's all a whine and the same complaint
over and over again, what difference do details make?
 When I was happy, my work was happy, but now,
sad, it's sad. One has no choice in this curious business.
 Of what should I write but the nasty, bitter, and bleak
countryside, life, and world I find myself stuck in and pray
 that I may not die in? It isn't boring to me.
The pain of others is not a compelling subject unless
 there's sympathy, understanding—whatever you like
to call that gift of the spirit. I try not to overburden
 the same people: I vary my supplications—
if the pitch is always the same, the mark is frequently changed.
 You don't imagine I've picked on you, alone?
Still, the critics are right: there *is* a dreary sameness
 to all these efforts. My reputation suffers—
which hardly matters. I couldn't care less. My Muse may be
                                                    dreary
 but she's honest, absolutely, a credible witness
whose truth, though plain, should carry a certain moral weight.
 I haven't been sitting here shuffling poems to make
an attractive collection; I write these letters to friends to complain,
 or beg, or weep . . . I heap them up in a pile.
any which way, to help my cause or pay homage to others,
 a dying man, bundling up his papers.

Book IV

IV, 1 To Sextus Pompeius

Accept in tribute this poem from one who owes you, Pompeius,
    not just a couple of pages but his whole Book
of Life. Allow me, too, to use your name, to address you
    openly, thus—though it put me further in debt.
Say you prefer me not to, and I shall apologize
    at once, although the message, already sent,
may have won a degree of approval. My heart is full
    and cannot be restrained. I'm troubled that all these pages
nowhere display your name. It's hardly through oversight.
    Time and agin, I've written it down and crossed
out what I'd put there, and then felt awful, a cowardly ingrate.
    "Let it stand," I have said aloud. "Let him
see it. What if he does complain? My shame can't be
    increased from what I feel for my backwardness
in declaring how much I owe him." And that is the gods' truth—
    that even if I were to drink of the waters of Lethe,
which wipe the heart clean and smooth as a new wax tablet,
    I couldn't forget how much you have done to help me
or how much I owe you. Do not refuse in contempt this trifle
    I give on account. It is large and rich in impulse:
I'm willing to run the risk of causing you whom I owe
    displeasure. Willing or no, you must suffer my thanks.
Never before has your favor failed me. I can't think now
    you'll turn your back who have opened your purse and heart
even before I managed to ask for help. In disgrace
    and exile, I still rely on you, knowing how every
man is a kind of artist, a maker. And in your life's
    atelier, I am still the work on the easel.
Having figured that out, I count on you not to desert me now.
    As Apelles, the painter of Cos, is famous
for the Venus he did with the silver spray of the sea's glisten
    upon her hair; as Phidias' noble Athena

of bronze and ivory guards the citadel's gate; as Calamis
    claims renown for those startling horses one swears
must be breathing; as Myron is famous for cows; so I
    am known as the masterpiece of Sextus' genius.

IV, 2   To Severus

Severus, great bard who sings the doings of kings,
    what you are now reading comes from the land
of shaggy Getae. The letters we have hitherto exchanged
    have not been metered mail, which is rather a shame.
You should be one to whom I address myself in verses,
    for I should take pains and offer the best I have
in recognition of your unstinting care and attention—
    not that you need what you yourself can compose.
Who would presume to give honey to Aristaeus?
    Or who would offer Falernian wine to Bacchus;
grain to Triptolemus; fruit to Alcinous? You have a fertile
    imagination you cultivate with a steady
craft, so that your yield is the envy of every farmer
    in Helicon's valley. For me to dispatch verse
to you is presumptuous, silly, like sending leaves to a forest.
    That thought has stayed my hand as has the other
darker one—that my hand is not what it was, the talent
    tired and stale, the spirit battered. I plow
a barren shore with a blunted share that has no bite.
    You have seen springs silt has clogged so the water
is choked and cannot run—my mind is like them: the silt
    is misfortune's insidious muck and I am strangled.

If Homer himself had been carried and dropped here by some ill
                                   wind,
     even he would have struggled, gargled in Getan,
his gift going, gone. I hate to complain, but can do
     little else. I can coax from the Muse no smile
from the old days when we romped together like happy children.
     We glare at each other, a mismatched married couple,
enraged, wary, and hostile. I sit at my writing table,
     but she won't approach except with a dead hand
to stay my own and show me how far short I have fallen
     from better days. Writing is no more pleasure;
the satisfaction of fitting my sentences into meter
     is no longer a comfort. Indeed, my ruin
came at a writing desk like this one. And nobody reads
     these lines I labor to fashion—I dance in darkness
at a school for the blind. The Coralli with yellow hair and the
                                     other
     odd tribes of the Danube have no idea
what poetry is; they have only the vaguest notion of language.
     But what else is there for me to do, how else
can I get through the exquisite agony these hours
     inflict out here. Take to drink? Gamble?
I don't have the stomach for either. And gardening's quite out—
     you can't hoe with a sword in your other hand.
There's nothing but this cold comfort, the effort of which is
                                   familiar.
     The Muses do better on your account and offer
a life and a living too. I send my congratulations.
     In return I ask you to send me some recent work
so that I may delight in the notion that poetry sometimes succeeds.
     I trust that I still remember how to bless.

IV, 3   TO A FORMER FRIEND

Complain? Keep still? Or if I do speak out, to whom
    should I address myself? Set down the name,
and make the son of a bitch famous? There is a tacky
    éclat, I'd expect, that comes from being attacked
not just on privy walls but here in the verse of a poet
    who once was not a nobody. You can
remember can't you, who used to hang out, hang on to every
    word I uttered? You lolled on my craft's sundeck,
but as soon as the water got rough, you beat all the rats
    in your flight to safety. Okay, some people are born
deficient in courage. But you pretended you never knew me:
    "Naso Who?" as if we had not been chums
from boyhood on, as if we hadn't grown up together,
    sharing our thoughts and dreams with each other. You
do remember your youth, don't you? You must recall
    the golden hours we spent together when I
was your only idea of the perfect poet! It is you own
    youth you're betraying here, your own life's best
moments. That Naso you claim you never knew is alive
    and well, or anyway better off than you,
for I can live with myself, can see my face in a glass
    and not retch in disgust—not that you've worried
a whole hell of a lot. Were you such a great pretender
    all those years? Or is it faithlessness now?
Either way you're a nasty piece of business—unless
    you bear some grudge that I can't even imagine.
One of us now can claim a legitimate grievance against
    the other, but I can't think what I have done
except to suffer. Did you turn away from that? Is pain
    so unattractive, old buddy, that three or four words
on a single sheet of paper were more than you could contrive
    to send in aid? It's hard to believe. Harder

is word I've had that you have been putting the bad mouth on me,
  adding your petty insults to those much larger
injuries I've endured. Jackal! Vulture! Swine!
  But there aren't names for such behavior—nature
is never that vile. And human beings ought to remember
  how their affairs hang by slender threads
that the slightest breeze can disturb. One who is now strong
  may be in a moment undone as ruin's maw
yawns abruptly. And knowing how this can happen you
  should take better care. Fortune is fickle, even
more fickle than you, compadre, and dances her dance
  with fancy footwork atop a turning wheel.
To whom will you turn when it's your turn, old pal? King Croesus
  couldn't buy off the Fates; Dionysus, the tyrant,
for all his power, could not keep fate at bay but ended
  his days teaching schoolboys and fighting stupid
hunger; mighty Pompey, flat on his belly in some
  fetid Egyptian marsh in the tall grass,
couldn't hide, and they found him and cut off his head. It's tough
  to imagine but these things really happen. Believe me!
Had somebody prophesied I'd be here on the black
  shores of the Black Sea, watching for Getae,
I should have recommended a trip to the funny farm.
  But here I am. When the gods themselves are mad,
there's no treatment or cure. Bear it in mind, old sport:
  the cock of the walk can wind up in the soup.

IV, 4   TO SEXTUS POMPEIUS

There isn't a storm in which the rain does not let up,
  and the sky's shroud fray at least a little,

nor is there a field so barren that nothing of use can grow,
    pushing its way through the brambles. Fortune hands us
hard portions, but somehow, deep in the package, it hides
    some consolation prize to diminish grief,
or at least to give us the strength to bear it. Here I am,
    torn from my home, country, and friends, wrecked
on this Getic shingle, bereft, but even I have moments
    of solace and wonder. Walking the beach alone,
I heard behind me the beating of large wings and I turned
    expecting some giant bird, but nothing was there.
It was just the wind. But something formed the wind into words:
    "I am he who knows neither time nor distance.
Fame is my name, and I bring you encouraging news—that
                            Pompey,
    your friend, is consul, and his year will be bright for you."
And then I heard again that beating of wings as the goddess
    departed, intent on her other errands. Dazzled
I looked around at the same sand and the same rocks
    that were much less grim as they glinted now in the sunlight,
and I prayed to another god, to Janus, who ushers in
    the year that could be my year and is surely yours.
You will don the purple toga and prepare to walk in the Forum.
    Your halls will be full of friends wishing you well
and suppliants with their pleas. You will visit the temples to pray
    and offer sacrifice to the gods from whom
you seek protection and favor for Rome—Jove and Caesar.
    The senate will rise to their feet in your honor and you
will address the assembled fathers saying the usual things
    but with style, with the grace that comes from sincere
                            conviction.
The day will be stately and grand, its customs and decencies all
    correctly observed and auguring well. Those old
men will hang on your words, their faith revived and their hearts
    freshened by your belief, and when you are done,

and have given thanks to the gods and to Caesar the senate will
                                                            crowd
    to follow you out of the chamber and all the way home,
and others will join them to offer the praise and congratulations
    you will have deserved—I grieve that I won't be there,
cannot enjoy first hand the vision of your great triumph,
    but must be content to imagine it all from this
terrible distance. It's one of those nasty twists that the gift
    that got me into this trouble allows me to soar,
to envision plausibly well these events from which my exile
    excludes me. It's all clear in my mind. I see
your face, your confident smile, your eyes bright with excite-
                                        ment . . .
    But will they turn, will they catch some glimpse of me?
Will you, in turn, imagine me out here? Will my name
    cross your mind for an instant, and will you wonder
"What is that poor soul doing?" If only that could happen,
    my exile here would be almost easy to bear.

IV, 5   To Sextus Pompeius

Go, you little elegiac wisps, floating
    my exhalations back to Rome for the learned
consul's eyes and ears. The distance you have to travel
    is very great—and you fly with uneven wings
over earth covered with snow so that landmarks are hard to see.
    It's dead reckoning all the way and slow
going! But you'll get there. All roads lead at last
    to Rome, and the house of Pompey is easy enough
even for strangers to find, close by Augustus' Forum.
    You can always ask the way—but take good care,

if anyone wants to know where you come from and whom
    you represent. Fabricate something, invent
a plausible name. The truth may not be risky now,
    but who can be sure? It's better not to take chances.
It won't, in any event, be easy to get to the consul.
    Once you have reached the gate, you'll find the threshold
probably guarded and certainly thronged. He's a busy man
    with weighty matters before him, the city's complex
affairs and those of its citizens always his pressing concern.
    You'll see him there in that ivory chair, splendid
with carvings. Beside it, you'll note the symbolic implanted spear.
    But he wouldn't be hard to spot without those props.
Men look to him for wisdom, as he looks to Augustus
    and Tiberius Caesar. What little time his duties
leave him, Germanicus claims by right of their great friendship.
    Still, should he manage to find you a spare moment,
he'll extend his hands, I'm sure, in affectionate welcome and ask
    how does your parent fare. You may say of me,
"He lives still, and his life, such as it is, he owes
    to you for the gift of Caesar's great mercy.
Again he owes you, for having smoothed the course of his journey
    into these rude and barbarous lands; he arrived
safely, his blood not having been spilled on the ground by some
    Bistonian cutlass. And yet once more is he grateful
for gifts in the lack of which he would surely have been reduced
    to pauperism. Therefore, he bids me declare
he's your slave now and forever. Sooner will shaggy mountains
    lose their fleece of trees; sooner will heaving
Ocean get rid of the ships that scurry across her belly;
    sooner will rivers reverse their downward courses
than he will forget the debt he owes to his generous friend."
    Having performed these Vergilian exercises,
smile for the people, take a breath, and as well as you can
    do your best bow, presenting yourself

199

as my gift to him, a token. Only accomplish that,
    and you will have served the purpose for which I made you.

IV, 6   TO BRUTUS

The page you now hold in your hand comes from a place
    you wouldn't wish on anyone, let alone
your old friend, Naso. But what have wishes to do
    with the ways our lives go? The Fates are willful
and deaf, as often as not, to prayers. I've now spent five
    years here, an Olympiad and more,
and every day have prayed my heart out. But Fortune is hard,
    moves not even an inch, and out of spite
won't let me move either. I've tried appealing to friends
    but again the Fates check me. Maximus promised
to speak on my behalf to the August god—but died.
    It's as if even the thought of helping Naso
were somehow fatal. I feel as though I were his killer
    and dread asking anyone else for the help
I need. It's not, we'll agree, a lucky business: Caesar
    had seemed on the point of issuing that pardon
I dream of here and live for. And now, with Maximus gone,
    my hopes are dashed. What is there left to do
but start fresh? I send you this poem, Brutus, to note
    with proper reverence Caesar's apotheosis.
Perhaps even this modest gesture on my part may,
    at such a moment, move the powers, gentle
what is now divine wrath, smooth the Olympian brow,
    and bring an end to the sorrows that gall me here.
I send my poem to you because we are friends and I know
    for certain you share my feelings and utter the same

prayers as I do here of praise and of supplication.
    You have been one whose love has braved misfortune,
ignoring my disgrace or defying it. Your tears
    matched my own—a stranger might have thought
we were about to depart together into exile.
    Your nature is kind; your heart, generous, open;
your sympathy, quick and sure. What's sometimes hard to believe
    is how you can speak in the Forum, as you are able
so well to do, on the prosecution's side. I've heard you
    speak for the law, your every word honed
sharp as a spear, with its dart a glisten of poison venom.
    And then you go home and are different altogether,
the real and almost excessively gentle man I know.
    Having endured the turning away of friends,
having heard their claims that they never knew me, their
                                volunteered
    insults against me . . . I've learned the hard way what
a real friend can be—and you are one. And I
    shall never forget you. In my worst moments here,
I think of you and from that thought take heart. The Danube
    I stare at through my window will turn around,
suck salt from the Black Sea, and will bring it inland
    before I forget those few of you in Rome
who mourned my exile, who think of me and grieve,
    who miss me sometimes—as I sorely miss you.

IV, 7   TO VESTALIS

You've put in time in these Black Sea backwaters, meting out
    justice to butchers: you know, then, at first hand

what manner of country it is in which I languish, can vouch
 for the testimony I give. Rome will believe you
when you confirm that I don't invent or exaggerate;
 I don't try to be funny but merely describe
what any man can see, or can't help seeing—the Pontus
 freezing solid, the wine in the wineskins freezing
so that the tavern-keeper offers to cut you a slab
 of his not-at-all-bad Pinot . . . You can remember
shaggy Iazygian herdsmen dragging their wagon trains
 across the Danube's ice that was thicker than they were.
(At any rate, it held them.) You saw the poisoned arrows
 and what they could do to a man. In engagements here,
that weren't pitched battles but nasty skirmishes, you
 earned your centurion's field commission and proved
your valor and worth. The Danube's greasy green was reddened
 with Getic blood your cohort had shed. Aegisos,
perched as it is on that high bluff, nevertheless
 fell at your approach. The story is famous
of how when the city's treasure was raided, Vitellius came
 from upstream to retake it and you made your
brave dash at those walls. Donnus, your great forebear,
 would have exulted to see his worthy descendant's
triumph there that the rest of the world beheld. Valor
 in war is not a virtue that hides itself.
The sun's bright blaze on armor is single-mindedly focused,
 admitting neither pity nor modesty. You
shone in grandeur then as the stones of the enemy fell
 thicker than any rain of a shower in hell,
and arrows, with heads poisoned in viper's blood, sang
 like gnats. Your shield was more furred than bristled.
Several Getan arrows embedded themselves in your helmet,
 their painted feathers looking bizarrely jaunty.
A few broke the skin and you felt the pain and burning
 but less than you felt your soul's hunger for glory.

So at Troy, we read how Danaän Ajax endured
    the frenzy of Hector's assaults on the Greek ships
drawn up on the beach. You, too, were fighting face to face,
    hand to hand, short sword against short sword.
It wants a Homer to bring those sweaty faces to sudden
    and vivid life and then let the lights go out
of their hard eyes as their bodies fall in a heap in the dust.
    Your exploits deserve better, but all I need
do is point in mute awe at the stacked corpses,
    the work of your sword. They say you cut your way
through human limbs like a man hacking a trail through thick
    rain forest. The other soldiers followed
the path you'd blazed, widened it out, made it a highway
    to victory paved in blood, most of it Getan.
Our soldiers were brave, but you were the Pegasus other horses
    only dream of, tossing their heads and flicking
nervous tails. Aegisos fell, and you shall be famous,
    for as long as men can read what I've written here.

IV, 8   To Suillius

At long last, your letter has reached me, my learned friend
    it's message sweet still and bringing me joy.
You profess your loyal friendship and promise to try to do
    what a friend can. For what more could I ask?
Even if nothing should happen and all your efforts fail,
    I should be deep in debt for your having tried.
The good intentions count—they're rare enough, believe me—
    and when their object is one like me whose ills
are as grave, and many, and old as mine, fidelity counts
    as much as love, for lesser spirits flag,

or forget themselves. It's sad, but that's how it goes more often
      than I could have ever believed. I'm wiser now,
and in my sadness better know how to reckon kindness
      I no longer blandly assume. Our kinship
enables a certain claim—but even on that I have learned
      not to presume too far. What can a father-in-law
count on (not to mention a stepfather-in-law)?
      It is enough that you don't make loud and public
complaint of our connection. Not that I've ever done
      anything shameful, though Fortune has treated me badly.
Remove my one blunder, and I am entirely spotless.
      The family's anyway good, equestrian stock
from way back. It isn't perhaps such a terrible burden
      you have to bear. But you make no complaint,
and for that I thank you, as deeply as for your offer
      of intercession. The god you propitiate
is the young one, Germanicus Caesar. No other altar
      is likelier than his. That generous spirit
you shall beseech for aid, and even my dismal cause
      will be no longer hopeless. A wave of his hand
and even at this distance the sails of my barque will fill,
      bellying out in that gust, and as my craft
moves I shall offer incense to the holy flames in thanks
      to him and to you. No huge temple, I fear.
I've been reduced from that kind of wealth. But my thanks in
                                   words
      will be as rich as any man's for the bounty
I have received. All one can give is all one has—
      one lamb or a hecatomb of bullocks.
But what can better befit men of public affairs
      than the praise of poets? Heroes and leaders of men
live on forever, as they deserve to, only in verse.
      Their virtues survive to instruct and inspire the children
of children yet unborn. Those monuments in the Forum,
      the temples and mighty arches, loom in the sunlight,

but the winds of night are wearing, little by little, the letters
  of their inscriptions, while these may live and endure
in the beating hearts of men for a thousand years and more.
  Where is the monument of Agamemnon
except on the pages of poets? What stronger or surer
  stele could one dream of? His enemies' names
and those of his friends are there; all his deeds, his forebears'
  and children's names, his manner of death—they remain
alive for us in verse. The Seven against Thebes
  and the story of Laius' house . . . What would we know
of any of that? The gods themselves live in the lines
  poets have measured out. Their battles and loves,
triumphs and agonies echo in songs that the bards intone.
  The dawn of time, Chaos, the Giants' struggles
against the Olympian gods and their fall to the depths of the Styx
  when Jupiter's thunderbolt struck . . . It happens in verse
for us to witness. The God of Poetry's gift is to let
  each of us feel afresh the awe the events
first inspired. The glory of heroes' exploits remains
  alive even after the heroes have died.
To the rite the priests performed translating the great Augustus
  to the place he deserves in the firmament of divine
and immortal beings, poets also contribute, our words
  shining like stars in the diadem of the god.
Let Germanicus know that I shall dedicate my
  talent—however much remains—to his
service. Being a poet himself, he may take it kindly,
  or anyway not despise the gift. Had his name
been anything else, he might have prospered as one of us, would
  have outshone us all, but he had more urgent
and vital duty to furnish the themes for other poets'
  paeans. I have no doubt he still finds time
to pick up the pen now and again, to keep his hand
  and tongue alive and in touch with his feelings. Apollo,

whose hand is equally skilled with the strings of his lyre and bow,
    favors Germanicus, scholar and prince, with a doubled
blessing. And for my part, I have had to learn
    new tricks, have become a soldier-poet,
buckle myself into armor, and take my turn on watch,
    my eyes peeled for shaggy Coralli and savage
Getae, but hoping to be relieved of this duty. If Rome
    remains closed to me, maybe someplace less distant
can be found where I could sit at a desk and at peace praise
    his deeds of war. Do pass the word, my dear
Suillius, adding your own prayer to that of the man
    who can all but claim to be your father-in-law.

IV, 9   To Graecinus

From where he must rather than where he would, Naso
    greets Graecinus and prays the good gods let
this letter arrive on the dawn of your first day as consul
    in the same hour as brings you the bundled fasces.
Your friends will walk by your side to the Capitoline Hill;
    I, who cannot be with you, send these words
of homage and friendship for you to tuck somewhere in a pocket.
    You know my heart would be with you on that day.
If only the Fates had dealt me a better hand, if the stars
    at my birth had been more propitious, or if the wheels
of my destiny turned more smoothly, that pleasant office of
                                        wishing
    joy and success I shouldn't perform with a pen,
but my lips would give the words the living breath they need
    and the punctuation of kisses, delighted and proud

as if we shared your honor together. While the senators thronged
     about you, I should have to walk on ahead
taking my place with the knights in the order of march, and
                             hearing
     the cheers of the crowd that filled the streets to see you!
Happy as only little boys know how to be, I
     should take a child's delight in the smallest marvels:
the rich smooth feel of your purple mantle of office,
     the intricate carvings in ivory on your curule
chair. I should hope to be one of that inner circle
     who go with you to the Tarpeian Rock to witness
the sacrifice you made, and as the victim died
     I should offer up my own thanks to the god
enthroned there in the temple, doing him reverence with incense
     from a full censer and heart, three times and four
rejoicing in your civic honor. I ought to be there,
     one of your friends, happy for you and Rome—
but I am forbidden the city. Reduced to a kind of blindness,
     I blink to bring into focus what's clear in my mind,
rub at my painful sockets, but cannot fray the darkness.
     The gods have decreed it so, and I must be
content, must accept their justice. Otherwise, we are all
     at risk, lost, each moment a free
fall in a moral void, a madness the mind refuses,
     holding fast to what it prefers to suppose.
It denies its exile and ranges home to behold your robe
     and rich regalia of office, believing still
in the justice you dispense. It approves your every decision
     as your bring beneath the ceremonial spear
the five-year plan's income and negotiate the details
     of public works. I imagine your splended speeches
and the senators' heads nod along with mine as you urge
     shrewd measures by which the state can better
discharge its duty and serve its people. I hear you tender
     the godlike Caesar thanks, and watch as you offer

the sacrifice of flawless oxen! And when those rites
    have been followed in proper form, perhaps you may add
one more prayer on behalf of your friend—that the emperor bate
    his anger. And as you speak those words, the bright
tongues of flame on the altar flicker and leap in apt
    omen for our oblation. And from that thought,
I take, even at this great distance, genuine pleasure.
    I have created my own festival here
to celebrate your year of consulship, after which
    your brother will follow to double your family's honor.
To yield your powers to him will hardly be to give up
    any, such is the filial love you two
share. Each of you takes joy and basks in the other's
    honors. The city's high regard for the office
you hold compounds with respect for the source of your
                                   appointment
    and the majesty of your sponsor. May Caesar's approving
verdict that elevated you and Flaccus for this
    service continue always. Let him confirm
his pleasure in how you conduct yourselves and the state affairs
    with which you're entrusted. Perhaps some idle moment
may offer itself, an occasion on which you may add your voices
    to the litany I intone year in and year out
in this awful and distant place. Then might the breeze at last
    belly my sails and loosen the hawsers that hold
my ship immobile, tied to the dock in these dark waters.
    Not so long ago, the commandant here
was Flaccus, your co-consul. He kept the bilge-green Danube
    safe, restraining the warlike Mysian tribes,
and taming the terrible Getae. He was the one whose valor
    and quickness recovered Troesmis. The Danube ran
red with barbarian blood. It's hellish out here: he'll tell you.
    Ask him whether I haven't reported correctly
the rigors of this place, the terrible climate, the fear
    we live with all the time but never get used to . . .

The savages paint the heads of their arrows in serpent venom,
    and human heads are trophies that people display
and even trade. Ask if I lie when I say the Pontus
    freezes hard enough so a man can walk
far enough out to sea to lose any sight of land.
    And when he confirms, as I know he will, my story,
ask how my reputation stands in this part of the world
    and how I have borne these extravagant tribulations.
They don't hate or despise me here; I manage to hold
    my head up most of the time, showing the Roman
virtues of strength and calm we try to persuade our children
    to acquire and practice, should need of them arise.
And modesty too—if one can ever claim that for oneself.
    Nevertheless, people think well of me here
where reputations have to be earned, where the enemy's presence
    is constant and close, and where brute force threatens
peace and the rule of law. Ask if there's any complaint
    by man, woman, or child of how I've behaved.
I've even become a sort of an institution in Tomis,
    a public pet. They haven't the vaguest idea
what poetry is but they know I'm a poet, show me a poignant
    respect, and try to do what they think is right—
I'm excused, for instance, from payment of certain local taxes,
    here and in several nearby towns as well.
They know and understand that I'm eager to leave, and want
    what I want even though they'd rather have me
remain where I am. I'm also known—I swear!—as a pious
    person, for it has been noticed that in my house
is a shrine to Caesar. His picture is there in a niche; on either
    side, the two who are closest to him, his chief
priestess and priest, his wife and son; and flanking them,
    his two grandsons, Germanicus and Drusus;
and his father and grandmother too, the next rank out. To these
    I offer incense and daily prayers. The whole

Pontus knows I do this and that every year, on the god's
    birthday, I rejoice, making as much
of a feast as one can out here. Inquire of any man
    who has ever been here whether I stretch the truth
or exaggerate in the slightest. Your own brother should know,
    having done his time at this hardship post. My means
are hardly the match of my wishes, but I do what I can.
    And not, as some suppose, in order to write
that these are the things I have done. At this distance from Rome,
    it doesn't cross one's mind to put on a show—
but somehow word could reach the ear of Caesar from whom
    nothing is hidden. That's possible, surely, now
that he is one with the gods, sees what goes on in the world,
    and from his place in the stars hears the prayers
of anxious lips. One day, these poems I write, which are
    a kind of prayer, may reach their perfect reader.
As one of his minor priests, I prophesy that the god
    will respond to one who addresses him as "Father."

IV, 10   To Albinovanus Pedo

My sixth summer on this forbidding shore grinds on.
    The Getae in fur clothing look as weird
as ever and smell worse. I have survived somehow . . .
    just tough, I guess, "as hard as flint" is the saying,
but even flint wears out; iron rusts; and stone
    gives way to water's constant assault. The shares
of a plow will dwindle to nothing, but I persist, endure.
    Death has turned against me and does not deign
to touch so tough a bird. Ulysses on his voyage,
    sea-tossed ten years, homesick, sick of life,

is the paradigm for a soul's woe, but he had breaks,
    times that weren't so bad on Calypso's island
on the couch of a goddess for six years—one could learn to stand it.
    He heard the sirens' song and, better than that,
tried the taste of the lotos, bitter but anodyne.
    It made him forget his homeland. Where can one buy
such stuff? I'd be in the market, however much it cost.
    It's not just an absurd conceit: I mean it.
My troubles are worse than his—look at these savage semi-
    human creatures that skulk along the shores
of the dull and damnable Danube! I'd trade them all in a flash
    for Laestrygonians. Cyclops, cruel as he was,
wasn't a patch on Piacches, one of our tribal chieftains,
    and local Swine of the Year. Scylla was nasty,
but we have Heniochae here, pirates who do more damage,
    sink more tonnage, and drown more sailors than she.
Charybdis was also unpleasant, but we have our horrid Achaei
    swarming the shores for plunder and making them worse
than they already were with their rocks and riptides. The land is
                                          bleak

    and barren here, no tree, no branch, no leaf
against the glare of the sky. The arrows are dipped in poison,
    and winter enlists on the side of the hostiles to open
the city's gates—or worse, with the river frozen solid,
    make them irrelevant. Enemies march across
without getting their feet wet. You don't believe me, you think
    I'm laying it on thick for rhetoric's sake?
I only wish I could make you see how it is to live
    from day to day in a place too bad for belief.
I endure hardships that surpass the imagination of any
    moderate man. But that's just the point: it isn't
moderate here at all. It's extreme, unruly, and mad.
    The inimical constellations here are close
so that one could think to climb a tree and reach out a hand
    to touch them—if we had trees, that is. The cold

pours at night from the rim of the Little Dipper. The winds,
    all from the north, howl and moan like crazy;
gentler southerly breezes don't even know how to get here.
    When one of them, lost and confused, arrives by some
mischance at this dreary outpost, it's weak, exhausted, and

                                     twitches
    and dies like a fish out of water. The rivers mix
and flow into this landlocked sea—it's a vast cesspool
    of the Dniester, Dneiper, Bug, Prut, Stredetska,
and lots more like them you've probably never heard of. The Don
    you know because it marks the end of Europe
and the start of the empty space of Asia. But where are the Ingul
    and Ingulets? Flowing through deep gorges, falling
in cataracts, and winding their way through a country
    where nobody reads Latin or anything else
(including maps) and the women pound their laundry on rocks.
    Legend claims that Achaian heroes explored
the Borysthenes, and clear Dyrapses, and gentle Melanthus
    that drift and drain and flow and pour and flush
into the Black Sea turning into a swamp
    or stagnant pool. Its color is off; its smell
isn't the bracing salt sea-air is supposed to be.
    In short, it's awful . . . But why do I write you this
dismal description? To make the time go by! To turn
    my back on the view and the terrible Getae and lose
myself in the friendly whiteness of an empty sheet of paper
    I can fill up with regular lines. It's soothing.
I'm sure you understand. You write about grander subjects
    and as you recount the deeds of your hero, your spirit
takes on a certain verve as you start to project yourself
    into the life you are trying to understand.
You become your hero—it's hard. No one expects you to kill
    the robbers Theseus killed, but you do take on
some of his moral excellence: steadiness, loyalty, love
    that isn't fickle and doesn't depend on fortune's

flighty smile. Your readers can learn such virtues from you
        as well as from what you write, as I can attest,
having myself had ample occasion to see how well
        you behave to a friend whose luck has gone bad. I read
what you write on the page, as I read the unwritten text of your
                                                    heart,

        with equal admiration and gratitude.

IV, 11   TO GALLIO

It would be, Gallio, dearest friend, a sin—of omission,
        but mortal I think—were I to fail to include
you in these lines of verse. When the god struck me down, your
                                                    tears

        were the balm that bathed my wound—A rich gift!
I only wish that loss of your friend had been the last
        exaction the gods demanded of you, but, no,
they are cruel and tax you further. The letter has only now
        reached me with news of the death of your good wife,
and now the tears that fill my eyes are for your hurt.
        I shall not try to console, condole, or repeat
words of the wise to one who is wiser than I am. That time
        is the slow healer, we know—and the distance and time
these letters have taken to come and go may prove the saying's
        truth. In the year that has passed, I trust your soul's
wound has healed, or anyway scarred over. To touch it
        at this late date might open it up again,
which is not what I want. I prefer to imagine you better, recovered,
        your old self, maybe in love again,
maybe even remarried. It may well be that the time
        for celebration has come, that I ought to send

delight, congratulations, a Health. My love you know
  you have, in whatever mood, at whatever season.

IV, 12   To Tuticanus

Your name, my friend—it simply will not fit in the meter
  to which I am now committed. Worthy it is
of honor—if any honor still attaches to getting
  included in what I write. But the elegiac
line won't take it: the stresses are wrong (unless I break
  the name and run it on, enjambing, which feels
like cheating a little). The only other solution would be
  bizarre pronunciations: TU-ti-ca-NUS?
Tu-ti-CA-nus? That almost does it, but isn't exactly right,
  and one of us would be laughed at—probably me,
for the lapse of taste. I'd run that risk, except that the point
  of the exercise would be lost, for you'd be displeased.
We've known each other for years, ever since we were little
  more than boys. Which prompts an idea—to invent
a nickname. This is a liberty we may allow a few
  very close and very old friends. I take it,
grab at whatever straws there are for someone who thrashes
  in trouble in deep water. Horace, I think
did it with place names. Is that a precedent I can rely on?
  Another thought is that I could send you the verses
for you to repair as you please. And if you're pleased, then I
  won't give much of a damn for the rest of the world.
You were my guide, my comrade. We read our earliest poems
  to one another, and talked of what we would be
and do when we grew up. I used to correct my work
  according to what you thought, and I learned what to do

from what you had done, polished and sure. I only wish
    I could, with as little trouble, also revise
the botch I've made of my life. The green of our youth so quickly
    gives way to the white of age, but nothing else
is sure—except our friendship. Adversity, time, and distance
    cannot conspire to blur the image of those
years when we were happy and had no reason to doubt
    that all our sweetest dreams one day would come true.
What heart, harder than iron, harder than diamond, is numb
    to memories such as ours? With total assurance,
I know that you often think of your beaten down friend . . .
                                      Sooner
    would peace break out and flowers bloom in the sunshine
of this desolate countryside, than you would forget your friend.
    Let me know how you are. Write me a letter
that will keep my hopes alive! I ask you this in the name
    of the god to whom you owe your honors and I,
my life. I'm like a vessel becalmed. A breath of hope
    is what I need for steerageway. Lose that
and I lose all. I languish. Just to get up in the morning
    becomes an impossible feat. To be able to face
the future is something that most men take for granted. Without
    that, the senses dull and reason goes.
I am holding on as well as I can, but I faint, fail,
    drown. Drop me, for pity's sake, that line!

IV, 13   To Carus

A greeting to him who is properly named—dear Carus, a friend
    in very truth. I send you a Health and a hug

from the end of the world. The style gives me away at once,
 not that it's necessarily good, but it's clearly
mine. Reverse our positions and I could probably tell
 what was your work, even without the title
page to announce it. A snippet without attribution declares
 with a burly but graceful vigor its authorship.
Your voice is perfect for celebration of Hercules' deeds:
 it's as if he had written himself into the text.
My Muse, too, has her idiosyncrasies, tics, and turns
 that give her away every time. Blemishes, maybe—
still, they proclaim their author. The easiest men
 to identify at Troy were Nireus, handsome,
and, ugly, Thersites. People knew right away who they were,
 as they used to be able to spot my work. And now?
It's hard to say. The saying has turned hard, and I stammer,
 revise, am never satisfied. I don't
hear Latin now. I confess I've recently sunk to a new
 low, have written a poem in Getic, setting
their grunts and gargles to classic meter. A joke—but on whom?
 The natives, at any rate, liked it, clapped their hands,
stamped their feet, and whistled. These are the ways they show
 approval: what they do not like, they kill.
My theme, at any rate, was noble: I sang of Caesar,
 invoking the god whose good will keeps me alive.
I explained to them how the emperor's body was merely mortal
 but his spirit wasn't, had soared up into its new
heavenly home. I told them how the son who succeeded
 is his father's equal in virtue. I told them, too,
of Livia, Vesta of matrons, worthy companion of husband
 and son. I taught them Germanicus' name and Drusus'.
And they listened, more than politely, nodding their shaggy heads,
 and when I was done and had folded the pages together,
they murmured, in Getan, approval, and one of them asked a
                                                    question,
 "How come you write of Caesar? You like Caesar?

He could, if he wanted, let you go back but he doesn't do that!
　　How come that is?" He waited, and I was dumb,
having no possible answer. Six long years I am here
　　trying to find that answer, in Latin, in Getan,
in wordless howls that echo those of the wolves in winter.
　　My poems are perfectly useless—worse, having got me
exiled here in the first place. I'd give it all up if I could.
　　The only advantage they offer is your friendship,
in the name of which I plead, friend to friend and poet
　　to poet: Do what you can. Speak a word
to Germanicus Caesar. Beg, in the name of his children to whom
　　you have been made teacher and guide that Naso
be given the answer with which to face the primitive Getans
　　as he bids them good-bye on his way to a better place.

IV, 14　　To Tuticanus

To you of whose name I have lately made complaint on the ground
　　that it will not fit in couplets, couplets come.
I am well, although not even good health gives pleasure here.
　　I pray every day to be sent anywhere else—
the Barbary Coast would be better; even the suburbs of Hell
　　would be an improvement. Gladly, I'd trade the Danube
for a snug shack on the bank of Styx. At least the people
　　traveling past would be lively and interesting.
As the tilled field must hate the wildness of meadowgrass,
　　as the swallow hates the cold it flees, I hate
this dreary town, or encampment, or call it a Getan foe-burg.
　　They know how I feel and what I write and send
to Rome, and they resent it—the Tomis Chamber of Commerce,
　　the Tourism Board, and the civic betterment groups

have threatened to break my hands, as a way to protect the town's
    image. It's hard to believe, but history has
repeated itself: my Muse has again gotten me into
    water that's more than tepid. I have to find
another hobby! My ship is driven onto the same
    reef where the timbers of old wrecks show themselves
and warn anyone with eyes and a brain of the obvious danger.
    Does it do any good that, this time too, I've committed
no crime, told no lie? It's hardly my fault that Tomis
    is chilly at times, that raiders do drop in,
uninvited and always at awkward moments. The landscape
    is not much to admire, and I have frankly
said so, but I've never insulted the people who live here,
    hardier souls than I pretend to be.
You have complained, yourself, of the countryside—the tradition
    goes back at least to Hesiod, who railed
at the grudging fields of Ascra, his own birthplace. And Homer
    allowed the crafty Ulysses, who loved his island,
to admit what was anyway clear, that the country there was rough.
    None of that counts for much out here in Tomis,
where philiopietistical passions run high among these
    clods who have no idea what that word means.
Metrodorus didn't much care for Italy, still
    we read him in Rome with delight and are entertained
by his wild carryings on. That doesn't cut much ice
    here, where there's lots of ice to be cut and where
they suppose a Metrodorus is some kind of subway exit.
    It's stupid, but then my whole life seems to be lived
against the not overwhelmingly clever grain of a world
    that doesn't change or ever get any better,
and I don't appear to be able to make the required adjustment.
    I haven't done anything wrong, I haven't attacked
anyone here, but have said how my own people in Sulmo
    couldn't have been any kinder to one in need

than those in Tomis have proved themselves to be. I am proud
    of the honors these people bestowed on a man they knew
had not just blown into town of his own free will. They made me
    exempt, because I'm an artist, from certain taxes
(unprecedented here but there hasn't been much occasion).
    They have placed upon my reluctant brow their sacred
chaplet. It's Delos to my Latona, the only
    place I've got, a refuge and sanctuary.
In exile from my native land, I was able to find
    a welcome here and a kind of peace for which
I am grateful—despite the fact that I have sometimes prayed
    that the gods had dealt me another and better hand
and issued a *carte de sejour* for a less distant and frigid
    outpost of what I had thought of as civilization.

IV, 15   TO SEXTUS POMPEIUS

If anyone's left in Rome who hasn't forgotten who
    I am, or wants to know how it goes with Naso,
let him know I'm alive and owe my life to the Caesars,
    but my health, I owe to Sextus who, after them,
ranks first in my regard. There has hardly been an hour
    in this long and wretched existence in which I haven't
enjoyed some benefit, profit, service, or aid from him.
    Favors, countless as seeds of the pomegranate,
or grains of wheat in a field, or grapes in a vineyard, or olives
    on a grove of old and twisted trees, or cells
of a honeycomb, I have received from him—I swear and attest,
    whereunto I set my hand and seal
as I would on official documents. Count me as one
    of your minor holdings along with your goods and chattels,

as described in deed books: all that certain plot and parcel,
        with the boundaries traced, and the title researched back
to the first land-grant from X to Y in those dusty ledgers
        the registrar keeps in some county office building . . .
So I declare myself, by this deed of gift, to be yours.
        Now you can boast of holdings off in the Pontus,
which sounds exotic but isn't. Indeed, I should recommend
        you find some better storage place for your goods.
I understand that it's not a question you can decide,
        but you do have a voice and influence and can pray
to gods who are well disposed to one who has shown devotion
        and faith as you've displayed for years—going back
even beyond the time when you were a witness in my
        dismal affair. You did what you had to do,
told the truth, and let the proverbial chips fall
        however they would. And I fell here, and plead,
not that I doubt your disposition or friendship, but only
        as one who dips his paddle into a current
that rushes, in any event, in the way he wants to go.
        I hate to nag, try not to, pick up the pen
resolved to write on any other subject, but find
        my hand making the letters and lines that tend
in the one direction I cannot change unless I leave
        or am carried off in a box. But the kindnesses you
have shown me, I shall remember either way. And others
        shall hear, if my Muse can speak beyond these rude
huts and muddy streets, that I am as surely yours
        as if, in a marketplace, we had struck our bargain.

IV, 16   TO AN ENEMY

What kind of jealous monster would make snotty remarks
        about the verse of the poor and ravished Naso?
Aren't you even a little worried that when you die
        a judgment day may come—and genius will get
what it has always deserved, as you will also get yours,
        my not at all good man. My fame will outlast
my failing body. When I am dead, it will rise from my ashes
        to thrive and prosper. I used to have a name
that counted for something, was counted with those of
                                        Marsus, Rabirus,
        and Ilian Macer, and Albinovanus Pedo,
and Carus. Look in anthologies, look in the textbooks and there
        I still am, and schoolboys learn how to count
syllables out on their fingers, measuring feet from the lines
        that I wrote. Look up my name in the index
and there you will find me, still at home, with my old friends
        Severus, both of the Prisci, elegant Numa,
Montanus, and dear Sabinus, whom I remember so well . . .
        He wrote the plaintive letters that wily Ulysses
ought to have written and mailed to Penelope home in the palace
        during those ten years he spent on his travels.
A wonderful poem that, but he had embarked on another
        on the battle here for Troesmis, which his untimely
death interrupted. Largus, whose talents were large,
        I also remember well; and Camerinus,
who sang of what Troy was reduced to, after the death of Hector;
        and Tuscus who wrote the wonderful *Phyllis*. They all
were friends, companions, colleagues, people whose judgment I
                                        trust.
        When my spirits are failing, my courage exhausted, my heart
ready to break, I think how all those talented men
        thought well of me and my work. One or another

might have been merely polite, but all of them, all the time?
    I reckon their names and work and talents and take
the courage I need to go on. The bard of the sea and of sailors,
    and the soldier-poet who only wrote of battles,
I knew them both, as I knew Marius, who could perform
    in any voice and in any stanza form,
and Trinacrius, his friend, who wrote the *Perseid*. We
    would all have a glass of wine, or more likely several,
and swap stories. It's not a thing that people would fake!
    Lupus and Rufus, Melissus, Varius, Gracus,
Proculus, Passer, who did those marvelous eclogues, and burly
    Grattius . . . How can I think they would all conspire
to suffer a fool? I rehearse their names as a kind of prayer.
    Fontanus! Capella, who wrote lithe elegiacs!
Though the list is far too long already, I cannot omit
    Cotta Maximus, noble on both his mother's
and father's sides. And every one of them read and approved
    of what I wrote. Therefore, I charge you, check
your malice and leave me to nurse my wounds that are deeper than
                                                     any

    trivial pest like you can dream. I am dead!
What satisfaction is there, inflicting upon me a new—
    if you could find a bare place to do it—bruise?

IBIS

For Hannah

In all my fifty years and hundreds of pages, I never
      stooped to write simply to wound; I never
hurt a soul, except, of course, myself. I dipped
      my quills not in the blood of victims but only
civilized ink. The time, however, has come to make
      an exception to my high-minded rule and attack,
or rather counterattack, that scurrilous man who will not
      leave me alone but jokes at my expense,
thrusting bravely at one who is innocent, helpless, exiled . . .
      And then, to outdo himself, he turns on my wife,   10
who has never offended, never done anything but suffer
      and weep for her husband's living corpse. This man
supposes he's safe because I've been sent as far from Rome
      as maps go. He thinks that I huddle here
in the icy nest where the North Wind's fledglings learn to soar,
      scream, and slash with their tiny talons. I do,
but my fingers still move, and I've learned how to keep my inkwell
      close to the candle flame so the ink won't freeze.
One discovers how to survive. A shipwrecked sailor, I grab
      whatever flotsam I can—but this man wants   20
to snatch from me those paltry pieces of waste lumber
      that keep me afloat. He knows I am poor but figures
the poor are helpless, natural victims and easy marks.
      What he forgets is that I am not the despised
and altogether defenseless target he takes me for.
      That I am alive at all is a sign of the favor
Augustus has shown me; my citizenship is still in effect;
      my property wasn't forfeit; and my work,
which has a life of its own, hasn't been barred from the city
      it's author can visit only in dreams and will always   30
love. I thank Caesar, as I often have done before,
      and beg he may allow me to move to a nearer
and less rigorous place. But you, villain, thug,
      and coward who kicks the fallen, I shall remember,

wherever I am, and your vile behavior. As long as you live,
    you may rely on my unswerving hatred
and vitriolic contempt. Water and fire will turn
    chummy; day and night will mix and blend;
the cold North Wind and the hot South will blow together
    in puzzling harmony; the acrid smoke   40
of Eteocles' funeral pyre will mix with that of his hated
    and hating brother, Polynices, before
I shall forget who you are and why I ought to continue
    my detestation of many year's standing. Whenever
I hear the howling of wolves for helpless sheep, I shall think
    of you and the tender place just under your chin
where the vein pulses beneath the skin that one might tear
    and slash . . . and like those wolves I'll sit on my haunches,
in wait for the right moment. Don't suppose that poems
    are all I have in mind. This is a warm-up,   50
or maybe a warning shot. As the soldier tries a new
    spear, fresh from the smith's forge, in the sand,
flinging it once or twice on an empty beach, so I
    merely unlimber with these lines that are hardly
the limit of what I can do. In decorous elegiacs,
    I issue a declaration clear enough
for any cretin to understand. I shall not mention
    your hateful name or specify your craven
deeds, unless you continue, in which event my constraints
    shall no longer apply and my second volley   60
will be with sharper barbs that are dipped in venom—a local
    trick I've learned. You've heard of Lycambes? If not,
look him up. The point is that Archilochus, a poet,
    was supposed to marry Lycambes' daughter, but then
the prospective father-in-law had a change of heart and mind
    and married his daughter off to someone with more
clout at court. The poet, displeased, sat down and wrote
    a satirical poem of such withering insult

that father and daughter, disgraced, dishonored, and desperate,

                                                          slunk

    off somewhere together and hanged themselves.   70
That's what you've got to worry about; for now I will only
    imitate Callimachus, who called down curses
on an enemy whom he didn't refer to except as "Ibis."
    You, bedraggled bird, can be my Ibis—
and you cannot reply without identifying yourself.
    This is my New Year's wish in reverse, that you have
all manner of sorrow, pain, disgrace, and woe—
    as you deserve. I call on the gods of land
and sea and sky to witness and aid in this invocation
    and prayer—and any poem is also a prayer   80
with its special kind of truth. You, serious constellations
    wheeling about in the sky, you, sun and moon,
and all you gods and spirits of earth and the underworld,
    old as chaos or young and recently raised
to be demigods or gods, be with me now as I chant
    my imprecations against that cur as grief and rage
bubble up from the deepest springs of my hurt being.
    Bless my desires and grant my misery's prayers
so the words I utter may soon translate into events
    in the actual world; let him be richer in woe   90
than even I can imagine, fulminating and cursing
    from far away. Allow my spells to work
on him for whom I am using an assumed name, for you know
    who he is and where he lives. I pray
that whatever spirits attend me may hear and approve and will fly,
    as only spirits can, to wait on Ibis,
return to Rome in the wink of an eye and mark how the tears
    pour down his face. Greet him in evil omen
with the left foot forward and clad in funereal black.
    The procession is ready? Good! Let it begin.   100
The priest does not delay but turns to face the assembled
    congregation, bows three times to the altar,

signals the chorus master for the pious hymn to commence,
    takes a breath, and intones: "Offer thy throat,
O terrified victim, freely to me." He raises
    the shining knife and holds it high, as the rite,
awesome, dreadful, but beautiful too, is re-enacted.
    May the earth withhold her fruits from you and may rivers
keep their waters from you; may winds deny you their cooling
    breath; may the sun disdain to warm you; may stars   110
hide their twinkling light from your undeserving vision;
    may paths at your feet twist and writhe to trip you
and sea lanes heave in disgust if you are aboard some ship,
    fleeing, I hope, in exile, destitute, hunted,
and begging your scraps of food with a quivering mouth, and no
                                            one
    to heed your plea. May your body be wracked with pain,
and may you be troubled no less severely in mind and spirit,
    an object worthy of pity, whom no one pities.
May men and women laugh and rejoice to see you suffer,
    and may your tears inspire only contempt   120
and the hatred that I feel now. May every ill you endure
    only engender more, as rot draws flies.
May you pray the gods show to your hateful life the only
    possible mercy and end it—but may they turn
a deaf ear to your plea and compel you to keep breathing,
    even though your spirit writhes to be free
of the torture sessions your body's prison is still imposing.
    Mark my words, it will happen! The omens are all
dreadful, which is just what I'd hope: an enormous raven
    flew from the sinister side to augur ill   130
as I walked the rocky shore. I danced all the way home,
    sure that my spirit's prayer had been heard by a god
whose answer is cheerful for me but gloomy as it can be
    for you . . . I'm only worried that at this distance,
the news of your wretched demise may take some time to arrive.

But no matter, my hatred will surely keep,
pickled in gall and the brine of my tears. Whenever the news
    arrives, I shall make a celebration to offer
thanks to the gods for justice. As long as Thracians fight
    with bows and the Iazyges sally forth with spears,   140
as long as the Danube is cold and the Ganges tepid, my hate
    will continue to seethe just at the boiling point.
Not even death will end our ongoing war, but my
    ghost will walk the earth, laugh at your woes,
and mourn your moments of ease (I trust you will never know
    even an instant of positive happiness.)
Count on the fact that a bony rattle will one day chirr
    in your study or, better, bedroom, and fear will grip
your heart and shame your spirit, as a finger of accusation
    waggles before you. That will be my phalanx!   150
Whether I am undone by the passage of many years
    or take my own life one of these days;
whether I die in a shipwreck on the way home so that fish
    nibble my flesh, or some carrion bird out here
snatches at chunks of my corpse left out on this Asian waste,
    or wolves have torn me limb from limb and their jaws
are flecked with my blood; whether I'm decently buried or burned
    in a common pyre; wherever I am, however
I died, I shall burst the gates of hell, by the force of my will,
    to return to the land of the living and stretch out my icy   160
hand to grab your scrawny windpipe and seize revenge.
    Waking, you will behold me; asleep, you'll see
my laughing face, for I shall know, as you do not
    now know, that divine justice exists,
and people are punished, tormented endlessly. You will never
    rid yourself of your own personal fury.
Your hearth will spit sparks and the hiss of serpents will sound
    in your ear with a warning already too late
to do any good. Your torches and tapers will smoke and blacken
    your walls to match the blackness of your heart   170

and soul. And when you die there will be no funeral rite
for a death that is no one's loss, for your own kin
will be glad, and you won't have friends (you hardly have any

now).
You'll be unmourned, unmissed. At the hand of the public
hangman, more than likely, you will be dragged through the

streets,
a hook fixed in your flesh, to be burned at the stake
where the flame itself will shrink from a morsel so distasteful.
Or the ground will detest your corpse and vomit it back
into the air which will reek in turn, and the winds will howl
in complaint. Vultures shall pick at your bones on the

midden 180
and gag and spit out what even they cannot swallow, your bitter
heart having fouled the rest of your nasty self.
Wild dogs will roll in the sweet rot you become
(but not quickly enough). The Lords of Hell
will summon you to justice and you shall be given a sentence
to make Sisyphus call himself lucky and prompt,
Tantalus' laugh. You'll envy Ixion's burning wheel,
an amusement-park ride compared to what they manage
for you for the next couple of million lifetimes. The fifty
daughters of King Danaus toting their leaky 190
buckets will giggle together and point at the chore the masters
of Hades have set for you. Tityus, groaning
as birds gnaw at his liver, will shake his head at the worse
torments you undergo as the Furies tear
your flesh with scourges, hack your limbs to feed their snakes,
and cook your ugly face to a crisp in their ovens.
Your nasty ghost will be mangled, mutilated beyond
all recognition. Your own mother won't know you.
Aeacus and his colleagues on the bench of Hell shall devise
truly inventive tortures to while away 200
the slow creep of the endless aeons and, having died,
you will plead for death's oblivion, its precious

gift that is yet withheld from you on account of your sins,
       myriad, countless, more than the leaves on the trees
on the slopes of Ida, more than the waves of the Libyan sea
       that slam onto the shore, more than the blossoms
of the upland meadows of Sicily, more than the sharp hailstones
       of winter storms upon Athos. A chorus of thousands
could not begin to describe your defects or weep for the woes
       you have inflicted on others, but all those tears   210
will glisten at last on cheeks that shake with laughter to see
       how tears can also flow from your piggy eyes.
Your birth was unhappy—that was what all the gods had
                                        decided—
       with not a single star of the heavens propitious.
Venus was absent; Jupiter in the wrong house and adverse;
       Mercury crossed you; Mars was hostile; Saturn
was positively baleful. None of this could be seen
       for the pall of cloud that hid this panorama.
This was, at any rate, a day of woe to Rome,
       July 18th—when we lost to the savage Gauls   220
at Allia. This was the day Ibis was stuck with, the moment
       he picked to wriggle forth from his mother's womb.
Roused perhaps by the frequent presentations of arms
       of the neighboring legionnaires, and in need of the R
& R himself, he appeared on the African coast. An owl's
       mournful hoot greeted his first moments
with terrible portent. The Furies, meanwhile, hovered about
       to baptize him with drops from the Styx and anoint
his breast with venom of Erebus' asp. They clapped their bloody
       hands together thrice and gave him suck   230
on bitches' milk to drive him crazy; his infant snarls
       rang out over the city. They swathed his body
in shreds of shrouds they had snatched from funeral pyres of lepers
       and victims of plague. They gave, as a baby present,
a chip of flint for a pillow to tuck underneath his head.
       Then, before they took their leave, they bade him

fare ill, thrusting a greenwood torch in his tiny face
    so the smoke would make him weep, and one of the sisters
cackled, "Go on and cry. Cry, you little bastard!
    It's good practice. You'll never be without cause,   240
not till the day you die, or even then, for a prophet-
    poet will come along to torment your spirit."
I am that man, the very prophet-poet of whom
    the Fury spoke: what I set down on the page
I write at the gods' dictation. From me you shall learn of wounds
    the future nurtures for you—like tiny fangs
of serpents still in the egg but already quickened with life.
    Those eggs will hatch in time. In the still of the night
you'll think you can almost hear the cracking of distant shells
    and a delicate first hiss. But how can we tell   250
the future except in terms of what we know of the past?
    Your ills and woes will be no lighter, surely,
than the sufferings we read of in lives of the ancients. Attend
    to a representative sample from which we may start
our grisly calculation of what you will have to face—
    if the gods do not mislead me and lend their strength
to these fervent words of mine as I call down on your head
    all the hurts of Troy, of winners and losers.
Remember Telephus, him whose suppurating wound
    refused to heal except with the rust of Achilles'   260
spear? That should happen to you—but Achilles will not
    be there with his medicinal rust, and the wound
will go on stinking. Or think of Philoctetes, whose heel
    the serpent had bitten—and it wouldn't heal either;
it smelled so bad that the Greeks banished him from their camp.
    That should happen to you. Or Bellerophon!
Think of him who was thrice victorious, so proud he
    tried the winged horse and was thrown to earth,
hurt and disgraced. He wandered, broken, the saddest
    of all mankind (except, of course, for you).   270

I give you Phoenix, whose own father blinded him, groping
     his timorous way, a step at a time, and mouthing
curses. That should happen to you. Or take another
     and better known blind man, the king of the blind,
Oedipus, whose daughters had to become his guide-dogs.
     Tiresias? Him, you know. But Phineus, pilot,
who taught the Argonauts how to get through that narrow channel
     between the Symplegades? Him too—struck blind!
And Polymnestor, let's not forget him, whom the Trojan
     women blinded with hatpins, jab, jab, jab!   280
Try that on for size. How does it look! I'm sorry,
     you'll have to take my word for it won't you? Fine!
Or something a little different? Dismemberment perhaps?
     As Saturn chopped up Uranus, I pray you may be
hacked to pieces, or torn apart by teams of horses
     as happened, I do believe, to the King of Alba
when he broke his treaty with Rome. Or Priam, whom Achilles'
     son stabbed, beheaded, and then sliced into
smallish bits he threw to the scavenging dogs—and that
     should happen to you! Or maybe a long fall,   290
where all the way down you know you're about to flatten and
                                      spatter,
     making a mess on the rocks. Thessalus leapt
from Ossa's height that way. Eurylochus was eaten
     alive by a nest of serpents—that would be good.
Minos was scalded to death when Cocalus' daughters poured
     those vats of boiling water down on his head.
That could happen to you. Too plain? You prefer flair?
     Prometheus, tied to a rock, suffered those eagles
ripping his vitals out, but that's not likely, is it?
     A safer bet would be something like what happened   300
to Philip of Macedon, who made improper advances
     to a young man he thought would be receptive.
That object of his affections pierced him all right, but not
     the way he'd hoped—he wasn't expecting a spear.

Irony, right? And amusing—if that could happen to you!
    Philip's son, Alexander, also suffered
a ghastly death, his guts tied into knots by poison.
    That could happen to you, but better, I think
of Achaeus, whose little rebellion Antiochus put down.
    Antiochus had him beheaded and then the body   310
sewn up into the skin of an ass and hung on display
    down by the riverside . . . But you don't have
the organizational skills rebel leaders require.
    Think, then, of Pyrrhus, King of Epirus, who died
when a flying tile caught him up-side the head, for that,
    at any moment, could happen to you too.
Likelier, though, is the death of his grandson who drank the
                                                      potion
    with Spanish fly and jerked himself to death.
That would suit you! Or Leucon, who loved his brother's wife,
    made his disgusting proposition, shocked her   320
into his bed—and there, in shame she killed him. That
    could well happen to you. But it's too tame.
I'd rather your face were blasted away by the desert sands,
    as happened to Cambyses' soldiers. Or hot
ashes could consume you, as they did Darius Ochus.
    Freeze to death, or starve, or be sewn in a bullock's
hide like Hermias, King of Atarne, and carried as freight
    to a death in prison. Or killed, like the tyrant of Pherae
by his own wife who wanted to keep him from slaying their sons.
    Milo of Pisa was drowned, and Lycaon,   330
who cooked up human flesh, was struck by a flying missile
    Jupiter threw in rage and disgust (I'd like
to see that happen to you). And your corpse can be dragged back
    and forth by horses as Eurydamas' was,
or Hector's. Or horses ate Hippomenes' daughter, Limone,
    the adulteress—that could happen to you. Or the Greeks,
on their way back home from the war at Troy, in sight of home,
    when their vessel hit that rock at the harbor mouth,

went down together, fast, with all hands lost—and that
    could happen to you. But I'd rather you had a wound,   340
bad in itself but that also drove you crazy. Lycurgus,
    to offer one example, went berserk.
Hacking at vines, he cut his own legs off and then
    killed his son, Dryas. And when his people
put him to death, they did him the favor I'd like to do
    for you. May your mother be like Aegiale, the whore-
wife of Diomedes, totally shameless. Or Arsinoë,
    who married her own brother after he'd killed
her former spouse. Or forget your mother! Better your wife
    should be just as faithless as she whom Talaus wed,   350
Eriphyle—who killed him, as Clytemnestra killed
    Agamemnon. That "deadly blow and deep
within" should happen to you in the bathtub—your rubber ducky
    bobbing on the crimson tide. And may your wife
be no more gentle than Danaids lugging their sieves—who killed,
    without even flinching, their several bridegrooms.
May your sister burn with incestuous lust as Byblis did,
    and if you have daughters, may they be like Pelopea
to her father's Thyestes, or Myrrha, or maybe Nyctimine, hot
    for her own father. Let her behave as did   360
naughty Comaetho, the daughter of Pterelas, who trimmed
    her father's hair and thereby cut the endless
strand of years that Neptune had promised him. The wife
    of Tarquin the Proud once drive a wagon over
her father's corpse—as your daughter, I hope, will do for yours.
    Oenomaus, you will remember, raced
with suitors for his daughter's hand, which was entertaining.
    The best part was that anybody he beat,
he'd kill and cut off their feet and their heads and stick them up
    on the gates of Pisa as ghastly tropies. At length,   370
somebody came along who beat Oenomaus, who promptly
    (but not promptly enough) did away with himself.

That would be good for you. Or think of his charioteer,
 the traitorous Myrtilus, Pelops threw in the sea.
What's hard to decide is whether I want to assign you the center
 of my guignol stage or let you be one of the supers
whose death is of no importance to anybody but you
 (who therefore resent all the more the way your life
is being thrown so lightly away). You could be one
 of those many unfortunate youths who got consigned 380
to the Minotaur's lair, or one of the dozen random Trojans
 Achilles killed in order to deck their bodies
on his friend Patroclus' pyre. The names are forgotten of all
 who couldn't respond right to the tricky riddle
the Sphinx had posed, but I can imagine their chilling screams
 as they fell from the high cliff she threw them over.
You could be one of the faceless, nameless victims in some
 bloody and general carnage with which you had little
or nothing at all to do. I like that a lot, and think
 of those other Trojans who fled to the Temple of Siris 390
in the hope of divine protection. Minerva was pained to see them
 butchered there where they lay on her marble floor—
which is why the goddess is represented as always veiled.
 (If you had been one of the victims, she'd have peeked
for a satisfactory glimpse.) Diomedes fed his mares
 on human flesh, but we do not know the names
of the sons and daughters and husbands and wives, all fodder.
 I'd be delighted if you were part of that mash.
Therodamus liked to feed passers-by to his lions;
 Thoas would use them as victims for sacrifice 400
to Artemis. You could be one of those travelers. You could be
 one of the sailors whom Scylla grabbed, or Charybdis,
whom Polyphemus ate, whom the Laestrygonians threw
 into their cannibal pot. You could be one
of Penelope's handmaidens who cast their lot with the suitors
 so that Ulysses, returning, killed them all.

You could be one of those people Antaeus wrestled to death
    before Hercules came along, or some
stranger whom Periphetes clubbed to an ugly death
    before Theseus happend by. Another   410
ogre Theseus killed was Pityocamptes who bent
    pine trees and tied his victims to them to see
how, when the trees snapped back, their bodies would burst apart.
    You could be one of those demonstration subjects
on a list no one remembers and no footnote records.
    Is that what I want? Or would I prefer you to be
an object of earned contempt, or a figure of fun like the Greek,
    Achaemenides, whom Ulysses put ashore
at Sicily for Aeneas to find later on, starving
    and out of his mind. Or Irus, the beggar, who haunted   420
bridges as beggars are wont to do (but you could be waiting,
    a kind of apprentice beggar, for someone to die
so that you could have your own bridge). I pray that Plutus, the
                                   god

    of wealth, shall ever be deaf to your supplications.
As waves on a beach suck sand from under one's feet, may luck
    melt your fortune that you can feel disappear,
pouring out through your fingers while you can do nothing to
                                   stop it.

    I want you to know want, your belly's gnawing
bad enough to make you as desperate as Erysichthon
    who kept selling his daughter to different masters   430
(and she would co-operate, turning into a bird, a dog,
    an ox, or whatever else the moment prompted).
May you be driven to peddle your daughter like that, famished
    as Tydeus was, who gnawed his enemy's skull.
I like the picture it makes—may you gobble the human flesh
    that Lycaon once attempted to serve to Jove,
or that Atreus dished out to Thyestes, or Tantalus offered
    the gods with his son on the menu, or Harpalyce

gave to Clymenus, that succulent *rôti de bébé*.

But that's not enough. I'd rather you were the victim   440
of savage violence, hacked in bits and strewn all over
        the countryside—as Absyrtus was, the son
of Aeëtes, Medea killed so that she and her lover, Jason,
        could make their escape. I'd like a new Perillus
to cook you alive in one of his bronze bulls so the roars
        of your pain as you died would resonate and echo
along the palace hallways, an ephemeral *objet d'art*.

        Or better, you could conspire in your own
painful end the way Pelias did, whose daughter persuaded
        the poor old guy that his manhood would be restored   450
if he let them boil him a while in a cauldron—he jumped right in
        and died. I think of the moment (it must have been early)
when he realized that he had made a foolish and fatal mistake,
        that knowledge being the pinch of salt in the kettle
that gives it a tang, a zest. But the best sauce for your goose
        is hatred, your own kindred's detestation
as revealed in their darkest curses. I pray for a bloody
        and painful end in which your family takes
satisfaction, or even a crazy kind of elation—
        as Theseus took in Hippolytus bloody end,   460
those rocks on the beach spattered red. I like the picture,
        that action-painter's mess. Osirus was mangled
by Typhon, I think, and therefore his sacrifices are made
        without the use of the blade he hates, which means
that the rites tend to be messy as they club their victims to death.
        Something as clumsy as that should happen to you!
Those victims are beasts, but you could become a beast.
        It wouldn't be much of a reach. Hippomenes
and Atalanta were turned to lion and lioness: you,
        less grand, would be a jackass, hyena, or pig.   470
Maybe you could be put to sea in a little box
        as Perseus was with his mother—but your frail craft

could go down almost at once, while those on shore (I include
    myself in the crowd) could watch it going under.
Or like Callimeles, you could be put to a picturesque death,
    buried alive. Or stoned, the way the Ephesians
used to do to some poor bastard to end a plague.
    My only hesitation is that such victims,
being blameless, may find some compensation in Hades.
    I'd rather you were destroyed because the gods   480
hate you as I do, point their thunderbolts at you, and fling
    destruction down on your head that you've deserved—
Capaneus, Aesculapius, Semele, all
    come to mind at once, or Phaethon. You
would enjoy a rarefied company, but that's the trade-off: divine
    violence comes with a dignity I'd be willing
to let you bask or writhe in. But there is a way to be violent
    and altogether undignified—if beasts
do the deed, if you're torn apart by savage dogs
    as Trasus was, or Actaeon; or if you're bitten   490
by a snake the way Eurydice was. You could fall asleep
    dead drunk as Elpenor was, and fall
to another kind of death as you roll over a ledge
    and smash on the rocks below. You could hide in a cave
as Cacus did and quake with fear as the cows you've rustled
    give you away by mooing (and Hercules came
and strangled him to death). If that were to happen to you,
    I'd have a drink and do a little jig
of thanks and joy. Or maybe you could make some mistake,
    a fatal mistake, of course, as Aegeus did   500
with his son's sail—and he threw himself off that high cliff.
    That's a good way to go! Astyanax, Hector's
son was thrown off a cliff, and Ino, and clever Perdix,
    whose uncle, Daedalus, jealous, flung him off
that tower. But no, I think I prefer the beasts—Phalaecus
    was mauled to death by the lioness whose cub

he'd stopped to pet; and Ancaeus, the Argonaut, was gored
    by a wild boar they were hunting. And there's a tale
I've always liked of the hunter who killed a boar and hung
    its head up in a tree, and then he took a snooze   510
under the tree. Diana, angry that he had failed
    to offer his thanks to her for his little triumph,
let him have his trophy all to himself—and it dropped
    out of the tree and fell on him and killed him.
That could happen to you! I also remember the story
    of Scopas' dinner party: Simonides
was there as one of the guests, was called away for a moment—
    some pressing piece of business, or was it Fate,
flaunting her clumsiness? And the house collapsed on the heads
    of Scopas and all the others. In that rubble   520
yours could be one of the names on the fancy place-cards. Or
                                  better,
    you could be the dinner, as Penalippus'
head was for the peckish Tydeus. You could cook
    yourself, as Broteas did, after his father,
Jove, had blinded him, and he stumbled into the fire
    and roasted to death. But that may be too quick,
too easy a way to go. I think of Callisthenes,
    who chronicled Alexander's wars but the king,
suspicious or displeased, had him locked up and tortured
    slowly, drawing the suffering out and keeping   530
the poor sod alive—and then they gave him poison,
    but one that took its time to do its work.
I like that, but its opposite also has an appeal:
    you could, like Eupolis, die on your wedding night
at the moment you least expect. But I want shame; I need
    the hatred I feel and the rage to show themselves,
and not from a distance, but close, from your own blood kin,
    or the kin of those you've hurt, as happened with Dirce
when Amphion and Zetus, her twin stepsons, dragged her body,
    living at first and then a senseless piece   540

of deteriorating meat, along the stony beach
    behind a chariot's wheel. That would suit
nicely. Pentheus, too, was torn into little bits,
    and Philomela's story comes to mind
with its striking image—her tongue cut out and thrown
    down on the floor to quiver a while at her feet.
Cinna was torn in pieces by an angry mob that got
    the wrong Cinna—they looked for Cornelius Cinna,
the one who had played a part in Caesar's murder, but any
    Cinna on that dark night would do, or be done to.   550
The old stories have more of a twist, an embellished turn
    the news rarely matches, but wasn't Harpagus
like Thyestes? Their sons were slain, hacked up in bits,
    and then the pieces were cooked up into a stew
they both were served for dinner. That goes the extra mile
    in the name of revenge, but I'm quite willing to take
whatever the *maître d'hôtel* is featuring. Strangulation,
    as happened, I think, to Theocritus, the poet
of Syracuse. Or flaying, like Marsyas, or turning
    to stone, as happened to any who looked on Medusa   560
vis-à-vis. Like Glaucus, you may be eaten by horses,
    your own, that you had specially trained to prefer
human flesh to oats. Or consider the other Glaucus,
    who thought himself a god of the sea and marched
down the beach and into—and under—the water and drowned,
    choking at last on mortality. I like it!
As a matter of fact, there's a third unlucky Glaucus—an infant
    who fell into a pot of honey and drowned
in the sticky stuff. That would be good. But your own son
    could have a hand in the deed, as Telegonus did,   570
Circe's son by Ulysses, whom he at last dispatched
    with a sting-ray's poison barb. That makes a nice
point, as Anticlus' story has its witty aspect—
    he was inside the Trojan horse, and when Helen

mimicked the beckoning voices of all the wives she had known
    of the Greek warriors, he felt impelled to answer
and would have cried out if Ulysses hadn't held him in check,
    with a firm hand upon Anticlus' struggling mouth.
Without having intended, he smothered the man to death,
    the uxorious hero whose end would fit you as well   580
as it did him. Or pounded into a fine powder
    as Anaxarchus was—I can see that
as absolutely right for you, but the reason should be
    trivial, petty. Remember how Polydorus,
Priam's son, was killed for the treasure of Troy by his host,
    Polymnestor, his brother-in-law? So you
may be killed for greed, but of something far less dear—those few
    copper coins in your pocket (all you own)!
I want your family with you; the whole clan should be there,
    as Damasichthon's was, and all wiped out   590
at one terrible time. And you ought to be the last
    so that you see and understand what's happened.
Better than that, you might, like Palinurus, survive
    the long swim, the grabbing waves that gobble
sailors and even playwrights. Your arms are aching and weary.
    You make it to shore, as he did, stagger and fall,
but somehow you haul yourself out of the surf and up
    the pebbly beach where you give thanks to the gods,
but a little prematurely. The nasty inhabitants swarm
    down from their huts to kill you for the poor   600
rags you haven't lost in your long ordeal. It's bad,
    but good for you! as Euripides' death would be
splendid: torn to bits by a pack of vicious dogs.
    For a son of a bitch like you, it has a certain
rightness. But there are other intellectual deaths
    I delight to imagine for you—Empedocles jumped
into the hot caldera of Aetna and sizzled or melted
    to death in the molten lava. That'd be good

for you. And Orpheus, proto-poet, torn to death
    by the ladies of Thrace, suggests another conclusion   610
to your ballade. I'd send you a shirt from the house of Nessus
    if I could suppose you dying as Hercules died
with his skin burning in pain, and no way to put out the fire.
    Milo, the wrestler, died showing off his strength,
pulling a split oak apart, but the tree snapped back
    and he couldn't free his arm. Something like that
would be good, as you writhed in pain but also understood
    what a dope you'd been and how it was all your fault.
Or maybe what you'd done could be less stupid than that.
    Icarius taught the Greeks the secrets of grapes,   620
how to grow them and how to make wine—and a crowd of
                                                    drunks
    turned on him and killed him. And then his daughter,
Erigone, hanged herself. That could happen to you!
    Pausanias, King of Sparta, starved to death
when they walled him into his house (and his mother brought the
                                                    first
    stone for the mason to use, to seal the doorway).
That could happen to you. Palamedes, falsely accused
    by spiteful Ulysses, knew that he wasn't guilty,
but did that make it better or worse when they stoned him to
                                                   death
    for treason? Worse, I suppose, as I hope for that   630
to happen to you. But guilt suits you better, and fear
    of being discovered, as Dolon cringed in the Greek
camp, afraid to be seen. A cough, and his life would end,
    like that . . . It is that terror I want you to know
that won't even let you close your eyes at night but shows
    your death a hundred ways every endless hour.
And then you doze off exhausted, grateful that you can sleep—
    and you burn to death as Alcibiades did!
Or maybe you die out here from one of the poisoned Getan
    arrows I worry about! It's hardly complete,   640

a short and hasty list, for the gods are inventive: their
    talents for pain being much greater than mine.
Adieu, then, Ibis: next time, your name will appear *en clair,*
    as it already does on so many privy walls.

David R. Slavitt was born in White Plains, New York, and educated at Andover, Yale, and Columbia. For seven years he wrote book reviews and film criticism for *Newsweek*. He has published ten volumes of original poetry, fifteen works of fiction (including, most recently, *Lives of the Saints*), and translations of the elegies of Tibullus and of the *Eclogues* and *Georgics* of Virgil. David Slavitt has also written two books of nonfiction and edited a volume of Adrien Stoutenberg's poems. He now lives in Philadelphia.